Stir What You've Got

A volume in
Identity & Practice in Higher Education–Student Affairs
Pietro A. Sasso and Shelley Price-Williams, *Series Editors*

Identity & Practice in Higher Education–Student Affairs

Pietro A. Sasso and Shelley Price-Williams, *Series Editors*

Working While Black: The Untold Stories of Student Affairs Practitioners (2022)
  Antione D. Tomlin

Stir What You've Got

Insights From a College President

William T. Greer, Jr.

INFORMATION AGE PUBLISHING, INC.
Charlotte, NC • www.infoagepub.com

Library of Congress Cataloging-in-Publication Data

A CIP record for this book is available from the Library of Congress
http://www.loc.gov

ISBN: 979-8-88730-139-6 (Paperback)
      979-8-88730-140-2 (Hardcover)
      979-8-88730-141-9 (E-Book)

Copyright © 2023 Information Age Publishing Inc.

All rights reserved. No part of this publication may be reproduced, stored in a retrieval system, or transmitted, in any form or by any means, electronic, mechanical, photocopying, microfilming, recording or otherwise, without written permission from the publisher.

Printed in the United States of America

To Fann, the love of my life.

To our family:
William, Robert, David, Carrie, Amanda, Rachel, Meade, Thomas,
Martin, Polk, & Watson who inspire us every day
and make our hearts sing.

Contents

Acknowledgments ix
Introduction xi
1 Changing and Shaping Lives 1
2 Small Town Roots 5
3 Sowing Seeds for the Ministry 11
4 Bonnie Scotland 17
5 Bridging a Racial and Cultural Divide 23
6 For Everything a Season 31
7 Andrew College 37
8 New Challenges, New Goals 43
9 North Carolina Bound 47
10 Grace and Gratitude 51
11 Knowing When to Move On 57
12 Knowing What is Expected 63
13 Humility as a Humble Servant 69

14	Collaboration and Relationships	75
15	Putting Out Fires	83
16	Stewardship: Why it Matters	89
17	Looking Back, Moving Forward	101
18	Where Do We Go From Here?	107
	References	115

Acknowledgments

Throughout my career many people have encouraged and supported me and I have experienced the same encouragement and support in writing this book. It would be impossible to name everyone, but there are a few people whose help I must acknowledge. They were scholarly, driven, and sometimes they pushed me to the wall when I needed to be pushed. Often times I dreaded their comments even though I respected them and needed to know their thoughts.

I'm thankful first to Connie Sage Conner, a gifted writer and editor, who worked hand in glove with me for many years throughout the writing process, raising important suggestions and questions while providing insight and encouragement. Susan Deutch provided provocative questions. Internet Technology specialist and "guru," Randall Bilbery, was a life saver on countless occasions. I am grateful to my colleagues at Andrew College, Brevard College, and Virginia Wesleyan University for their help and the wonderful memories that are the basis for this book. Virginia Wesleyan University's longtime dean and presently the university's archivist, Dr. Steve Mansfield was tremendously helpful providing dates, photographs, and experiences. Virginia Wesleyan University's head librarian, Stephen Leist, helped with photographs. Tyron Spearman and the late Dr. Frank McGill both knew Dr. Pete Donaldson intimately and related to me personal anecdotes and insights into his leadership style and the Southern culture he inhabited. A widely published author in the area of higher education administration, a personal friend and colleague, Dr. Joe DeVitis, believed this material should be published and encouraged me to share it with a wider academic community. Trustee, friend, and successful businessman, Lem Lewis, always recognized the connections between excellent practices in higher education and excellence in business and leadership. Dr. Larry Hultgren, Dr. Kate Loring, Dr. Terry Linville, Dr. Kathy Murlock Jackson, the late Rev. Jim Sell, Rev. Win Lewis, and Dr. Jasper Hunt all excelled in communicating. Unbeknownst to them my family helped write this book. The stories are our real lived experiences and the very fabric of our lives. William, Robert, and David, Carrie, Amanda, and Rachel, Meade, Thomas, Martin, Polk, and Watson continue to be my inspiration. All through this book I've written about relationships. There is no more important relationship than the one with one's spouse. Fann has been my partner in life, my confident, and my best friend for all these many years. She has been my constant encourager and editor throughout this process, and to her I give my deepest appreciation.

Introduction

In this little book, you will read stories about an average young man who grew up in a small, South Georgia town surrounded by talented teachers, coaches, preachers, professors and business leaders. They were role models and mentors for me and other youngsters like me. They wanted us to dream big. And we did.

They also taught us about the importance of relationships and collaboration. They showed us through their own actions that the world can be kinder, gentler and more just.

My hope is you'll think about the people in your own life who encouraged you and be reminded that your own dreams can come true. My life hasn't been a cakewalk, but as my grandmother taught me, "Stir what you've got." Use your God-given brain. Trust your gut. Be joyful. Laugh, especially at yourself. My journey hasn't been without its stumbles and disappointments—no one's is. We all have self-doubts, but most of us make decisions based on what we inherently know is right, even if it's not popular. Most of us like to think that the more birthdays we celebrate, the wiser we become. It has taken me decades to knit those experiences together into a framework of lessons learned to share with a new or would-be college president or anyone in a leadership role (or for that matter, my own children and grandchildren). My key insights: Life is not about prestige, accolades, and applause. It's about integrity, relationships, service, and collaboration. And I learned that we have to take risks, even if those around us think we're nuts!

After serving as the pastor of four United Methodist churches and studying under some of the greatest Christian theologians of our time, I walked away from the ecclesiastical life and into the world of higher education, exchanging clerical vestments for academic regalia. I knew it was time to make the leap and for me, it was the right decision. For nearly forty years, I had the privilege of overseeing the well-being of four colleges in three states and have watched a gradual shift in higher education marked by changing attitudes and a myriad of new responsibilities, issues, and concerns.

My first presidency was at Andrew College in Cuthbert, Georgia; followed by Brevard College in North Carolina; and later coastal Virginia Wesleyan College, now a university. After retiring, I accepted the interim presidency of Virginia's Eastern Shore Community College. They have all thrived and grown with my help, and sometimes despite my mistakes.

The segue from clergyman to college president is not as surprising as one might imagine. Each job focuses on being a compassionate leader, building relationships, shepherding and growing a flock, managing budgets, and guiding young people. A college's chief executive and a minister both need to communicate effectively, have good counseling skills, foster cultural diversity, and herald integrity, honesty, truthfulness, and objectivity. For me, a sense of mission was paramount.

I struggled with what seemed to be a preordained career in the ministry and almost an obsession with the receiving end of education, studying for years and earning two doctoral degrees. There is nothing earth-shattering about my life's path, yet it is unique in that I did both without climbing the typical academic or administrative ladder to become a college president. Having a theological background made me a better president. Perhaps it was not by accident that the two professions I chose also required being both a good listener and good storyteller.

As with the clergy, the focal point of higher education is service. I loved being around faculty, staff, and students. Humility and having the right values are essential to being a good leader. I had to be respectful, own my failures, and continually challenge myself, which could not be done without continuing to be educated myself. Those experiences led to community partnerships and collaborations with museums, entertainment venues, non-profits, and local organizations. The difficult part was finding the most significant and potentially rewarding and compatible connections and making them work.

What is the number one job of a college president? It is not, as some would have you believe, raising money. It's building, nurturing, maintaining, and monitoring relationships. That is the most important role of an administrator and frankly, of a life well-lived. I'm not talking about holding hands and singing Kumbaya; if relationships are not solid, any leader will be in for rough sledding. Busting up logjams are nearly as important, and quite often those bottlenecks are between relationships. Sure, there always will be people who are miserable and just plain soured on the world, but the amateur psychologist in me says they're really soured on themselves.

We all need inspiration, guidance, and wisdom. One of the things that is fast leaving us in this modern world is the old-fashioned notion that the fundamentals of one's life—friends, family, work associates—will endure. We are in the midst of an era where loyalty and commitment are eroding, which makes it all the more important for small- and mid-sized colleges and universities in particular to swim against a current that diminishes the importance of relationships.

As Mark Twain mused, the difference between the almost right word and the right word is the difference between lightning and the lightning bug. We can fail to use the right words and potentially erode cherished bonds with friends or colleagues. We're human, our judgment falters, and we get off track. We pick up the pieces, put them back together, and move on. Most of the time, I like to think I created momentum by understanding an institution's culture and by being credible, accountable, trustworthy, and by keeping my word to reinforce those ties.

My goal in these pages is to share whatever shards of common sense, sound judgment and values I've gleaned in the past seven decades. I credit the teachers, preachers, family, coaches, and friends who challenged me to reach beyond the borders of my small Southern town, inculcating values that are most important to me today, including my views about systemic racial, social, and political injustices and the power of education to correct them.

We can have a grand plan as we zigzag through life and it's going to go awry. Sometimes we strike out. Sometimes we hit a home run. I know from experience what it is like to be a good leader or a lousy one, be it college president or cleric. There are no magic formulas. As my grandmother used to say, "Stir what you've got." I tried to do the best I could every day and hoped it was enough.

It's a lonely world out there and sometimes there aren't many people we can turn to. Over the years, I've found it energizing and inspiring to read stories of women and men who have confidently scaled a mountain peak or painfully nose-dived into a proverbial valley and how their outlook on life may have changed because of it. The highest compliment someone could give me would be that they picked up this little book and that it pulled them into thinking about their own lives—how they've handled joy and adversity, and how they've related to people and events. Perhaps they'd say, "Yes, I know what he's talking about."

I am a Southerner and a storyteller, and by sharing stories—pearls of wisdom—as one friend calls them, readers might cull useful tidbits of what worked for me and what didn't. These pages are my negotiations with myself and the Almighty. Hopefully, you will find them helpful for your own life. As a wise Chippewa (Ojibwe) tribal leader told author Kent Nerburn, "Always teach by stories. People learn best by stories because stories lodge deep in the heart" (Nerburn, 1994, p. 188).

This is my story.

1

Changing and Shaping Lives

As educators, students are our primary focus. That's what we do—educate and mold students into what they will become. One late August afternoon as I walked through the Virginia Wesleyan campus I saw what looked like a family standing beside the statue of John Wesley, founder of Methodism. My curiosity was piqued, and I altered my route a bit and walked over to them.

"Who is the student in this group?" I asked. That was all the encouragement they needed to strike up a conversation with me. "We are on vacation," replied the older gentleman. "I attended Wesleyan in the late '70s. I brought my family here because I wanted them to see the place where I became the person I am today."

That response stopped me dead in my tracks. I began to reflect on how we teach skills for life—the intellectual, leadership, and practical problem-solving skills and the moral reasoning we cultivate and explore. I reminded myself again that we are more than a "filling station." We genuinely change and shape lives. There is no higher calling.

For me, being a college president was not about power and prestige, but mission and service. My calling to service shaped me every step of the way. It was early in my tenure at Virginia Wesleyan and on that summer afternoon, I realized how fired up I was about this calling, this ministry. I felt so alive and, at the same time, scared to death.

We live in a time when so much around us is being battered and bruised, especially by the unpredictable, be it war, climate change, politics, a pandemic, or rapid advances in technology. It is especially important that we have confidence in our institutions. As college presidents and caretakers we must be vigilant to constantly remind ourselves that as long as we appeal to some market (and we do) and watch our finances (and we do), then we will do just fine.

But I'm getting ahead of myself.

I had been the pastor of four Methodist churches in Georgia and the president of two colleges, one in Georgia and one in North Carolina, before assuming responsibility for Virginia Wesleyan. An interim presidency of another Virginia college would follow after I retired.

After a dozen years as a United Methodist pastor, I was beginning to feel suffocated by parish ministry. If I had 700 church members, I had 700 bosses. I've always believed I had to "feel" a job was right. In plain language, it was difficult being as religious as was expected of me. A parish pastor was just no longer the right fit. For years I had been drawn to teaching and college chaplaincy. Higher education seemed like a worthy career for many reasons—I could continue learning, I'd have a strong, supportive, and energetic team, I could still use my theological education, and I'd be working with young people.

My first presidency began in 1980 at the two-year Andrew College in Cuthbert, Georgia. I was six weeks shy of my 38th birthday.

I arrived at Andrew College's "Old Main" early that June morning as its newly minted, wet-behind-the-ears president. I'd passed through its entryway many times before as college chaplain, trustee board member, faculty member, and to confer with Jake Martinson and Walter Murphy, the two previous presidents who had become trusted friends. Having earlier served as pastor of Cuthbert's United Methodist Church for 5 years I knew the route well. But this would be the first time I'd walk these halls as the college's leader. My exuberance was overwhelming as I bounded up the back steps and into a dark hallway. A quick right turn, and there I was in front of the president's office—my office. I went charging through the door, past the secretary's desk, made a quick right into my office, and turned on the lights. I immediately felt at home.

The first thing I spotted on my desk, however, was the latest issue of *The Chronicle of Higher Education*, the bi-monthly newspaper for educators. The headline screamed at me: "Two Hundred Small Colleges to Die This Decade." I could feel white-hot anger surging through my body, and it awakened something from my past, something deep in my blood. It may have been the competitive basketball player in me, but I took this news as a challenge, one I was going to win. I snatched the offending publication from the desk, crumpled it, and in one smooth motion, slam-dunked it into the trash can and punctuated the action with the words "Not this one!"

I didn't know much, but I had a firm conviction that the people of southwest Georgia and bordering east Alabama needed this college. I would not let them down. Andrew was the intellectual and political hub, the largest employer and anchor for the surrounding communities in two states. Countless times over the years I had been in that office but had never felt the weight of the president's responsibility before that moment.

I may have been a greenhorn but I knew the faculty and staff were committed to the college. I could hear my grandmother saying, "Billy, stir what you've got because you have a lot to stir."

My maternal grandmother, whom I called "Mama Duke," lived in Americus, Georgia, and spent a lot of time with me. Once, as a small child, I was playing with my toys and whining that I didn't have enough firetrucks and firemen to put out an imaginary fire. She easily could have suggested we go to town and buy another toy. Instead, she put her hand on my shoulder. "Son," she said, "stir what you've got." In other words, use your God-given brain to figure out a way to snuff out that pretend fire. That bit of advice, one she uttered on occasion as I was growing up, has stayed with me throughout my life, whether personal or professional, visionary or tangible.

At Virginia Wesleyan, for example, we didn't have enough money to buy an expensive electron microscope for the biology department. Someone in the development office suggested applying for a grant. It wasn't rocket science but asking for a grant from a national foundation instead of a local donor had not been done before. We got the grant. And the microscope.

We stirred what we had.

2

Small Town Roots

My roots are in Tifton, a rural slice of south central Georgia some 50 miles from Valdosta along Interstate 75. The city of 17,000 is renowned for its world-class agricultural research. Nearly one-third of Georgia's prime farmland is in Tift County where generations have worked its rich, loamy soil.

Tifton also is a mecca for Southern hospitality—hardly surprising for a place nicknamed the "Friendly City" whose main thoroughfare is Love Avenue. It was home to the world's second-largest magnolia tree until it burned in 2004. Even the city park, whose dogwood and azaleas are a riot of white, pink, and deep purple in the spring, is dubbed Friendly Park. When people write or email the Tifton-Tift County Chamber of Commerce, they praise the residents for being cordial and helpful. It was that way in the 1950s when I was growing up, even though its population has doubled since I was a kid.

I was born July 28, 1942, the oldest of two children. Until I found out I wasn't. A full-term sister was stillborn. Her birth was such a well-kept family secret that I didn't learn about the baby until I was in my early twenties when my mother, Winnie Duke Greer, finally mentioned her oldest child's birth—and death. Jacqueline Jean Greer never came home from the hospital. There is no grave, no headstone and my mother had never mentioned her. I am struck by how little my family talked about such important things. I guess withdrawing and never mentioning her heartbreak was the way my mother handled her emotional pain.

My mother was born on May 10, 1917, in Reynolds, Georgia, a town not much bigger than a square mile. She attended Georgia Southwestern College and taught school for 2 years in Macon County. Georgia is nicknamed "the Peach State" and my mother's family, the Dukes, were peach farmers. In the early 1920s her family developed the first white peach they proudly named the "Duke of Georgia." They were ahead of their time. There was no market at the time for a white peach and it failed. But the idea of experimenting and reaching for something beyond the expected continues to intrigue me.

My mother, whom I called Winnie, was devoted to us and I knew she loved me deeply. A former teacher, she demanded perfection. If I came home with a paper with an A– scrawled on it, she would ask why I hadn't made an A. She sought to give me every enriching opportunity and expose me to beauty in many forms, including piano and voice lessons. But it was her mother, Susie Pearl (Davis) Duke, whom I adored. She didn't have an ounce of critical judgment toward me, and she's the one I called Mama.

I'm named after my father, William Thomas Greer, who was my hero and the smartest person I've ever known. Born on November 20, 1912, he grew up in Ideal, Georgia, no more than a wide spot in the road in Macon County. He was valedictorian of his high school class, and although he didn't go to college, he was a successful Georgia businessman.

My parents met in Macon County; my father was a state trooper and my mother was a sixth-grade teacher. "Big Bill," as he was known, was a tall, hulk of a man. In 1937 he was selected for the first class of Georgia State Patrol officers on Georgia's first State Patrol Force. Although he spent only a handful of years as a patrolman, he often spoke with pride of being assigned to guard and protect Franklin D. Roosevelt when he was in residence at Warm Springs, Georgia, where the president had a treatment center for polio victims and a home built that later became known as the Little White House.

My parents were married on July 14, 1938, and moved to Tifton a decade later. In addition to being a respected businessman, my father was a church and community leader, as was my mother, who was honored as the county's Citizen of the Year and honored with the Exchange Club's Golden Deeds Award. She was known for her many culinary gifts, especially her cakes. My father built an enclosed backyard kitchen for her with an enormous fireplace. Untold hours were spent with family and friends telling stories, while making up more than a few, in a big room dubbed "Sugar Shack," a popular song in 1963. I can almost see and hear those fires poppin' as they devoured logs.

"Big Bill" was a man of deep faith who read everything in sight. He was a cigar-chewing ex-Marine who wanted me to be an athlete. No one in our little town could throw a pitch or score baskets as he could. At Cub Scout camp, we'd walk off with all the blue ribbons in the athletic events. My Dad was competitive and he instilled that quality in me.

While we shared an interest in sports, I didn't know how he would cotton to the artsy side of my life. I had a decent singing voice, and in the fifth grade I was chosen to sing the solo in Handel's *Messiah*, "He Shall Feed His Flock" in the Christmas concert. At the dress rehearsal, my father showed up with a newborn lamb he had borrowed from a nearby farm. The next day, at the actual performance, the lamb was shaking almost as much as I was. Just as I began singing, the lamb let loose a long "baa" and the more than 1,000 people in the audience broke out laughing. The look on my father's face was priceless. My anxiety went away and I was filled with joy as the cuddly little lamb with pink ears snuggled in my arms. All felt right with the world. More importantly, just as I began singing, everything also felt right between my father and me.

On occasion over the years, I've been asked, "Are you Bill Greer's boy? Well, you and that lamb made my Christmas." Mine was the good fortune of having loving parents who did their best to challenge me and surround me with good role models and a strong faith community. Those relationships shaped my life in known and unknown ways.

My father owned a number of gas stations in several South Georgia counties. I began working for him when I was as young as 13. More than once during the summer, my mother would get a telephone call at 5:30 a.m., shake me awake, and tell me "Big Bill" needed my help. The service station manager had failed to report to work and it was my responsibility to step in. I'd get out of bed, throw on some clothes, hop on my Schwinn bicycle, and pedal across town to one of his filling stations where he'd been working since 5:00 a.m. "I've placed $50 in the cash register and when I come back tonight at 8 o'clock, that $50 better be there and then some," he'd say and head off to check on his other stations.

Today the term "service station" harkens back to a bygone era. But in those days I'd hear a "ding ding" as a motorist drove over the black rubber hose that was hooked up to a bell inside the service station and I'd run out to an old-fashioned gas pump to put fuel in a customer's car, watching as the little black numbers slowly turned to show the number of gallons of gas filling the tank. I'd also put air in tires, check the oil with a dipstick, and whisk Georgia's red, talcum powder-smooth road dust off windshields. The job was not very glamorous and far from intellectual, but as a kid, it gave me a taste for responsibility and taught me that managing an enterprise could be challenging and fun—lessons that I never forgot.

While my Dad had grown up in Ideal, Georgia, his childhood was anything but ideal. My paternal grandfather was an abusive alcoholic with all the heartbreak and shame that comes with it. Every time my father drove us the 90-plus miles to visit his parents, I could feel my own parent's anxiety as they wondered what they would find. My heart hurt for my Dad. He would ask my sister, my mother, and me to stay in the car until he checked things out. I could only imagine what he was feeling. As a child, I was frightened. I would watch him climb the front steps and disappear into the dark house, the wooden screen door closing behind him. Sometimes, he would wave us inside and the look on his face would say it all—Papa was sober. The visit would be a good one.

Years later, my father told me how bad Papa's drunkenness could get and the shame that continued to engulf him because of it. As he spoke, his eyes welled with tears and his voice cracked with emotion. It was the most in-depth he ever spoke about his father. As children, when he, his sister May, and older brother, Thurmond, heard their father coming up the gravel driveway drunk, they would hide in the attic. My grandmother tried hard to make an adventure out of it. Pappa would be loud and stumbling, knocking over chairs, and shouting profanities. Sometimes he would collapse, totally out of it. My grandmother and the children would scamper down from the attic at just the right moment to pick up Pappa and get him in bed where he would sleep through the night and most of the next day. That shameful alcoholism spewed poison throughout my family. I vowed to never live that way.

Though far from cosmopolitan, Tifton is a college town, home to Abraham Baldwin Agricultural College and the University of Georgia's College of Agricultural and Environmental Sciences, as well as its Coastal Plain Experiment Station, which includes 7,000 acres of research farms. Back then most of the public school teachers were women who were single or whose husbands had jobs in Tifton, often at the Experiment Station. The teachers' level of instruction was exceptional; as high as could be found at any elite boarding school. What I remember most was how inspiring they were and their ardent invitations for learning and growth.

One of my high school teachers was Mrs. Crum, a tall, stern woman with dark, penetrating eyes who reminded me of Ichabod Crane. She taught biology and Latin. One day when I was clowning around as usual with some of my buddies, she grabbed my arm and pulled me aside.

"Billy Greer, I want you to be in my college preparatory biology class next year." She looked at me intently. "You have a clear head."

I didn't understand what she meant at the time, but later realized she was encouraging me to take myself and my intellect seriously. It was one of the finest invitations I ever received. She was the one who, in my mind, sort of "discovered" me and had an inkling of what that skinny kid could accomplish. Mrs. Crum gave me the confidence I needed.

If other teachers didn't think I was up to speed, they'd also get my attention. One day after English class, Mrs. Mitchell called my name. "Billy, I want you to come back tomorrow and give the class a sermon as George Whitfield might have done." Whitfield was an eighteenth-century Anglican priest and one of the founders of Methodism. I went home and practiced and practiced. Mrs. Mitchell was trying to stretch me. She wouldn't have said, "Stir what you've got," but I would not have dared let her down. Those women were some of the smartest people in Tifton and intently worked at passing along their knowledge to us.

One of my boyhood heroes was Abraham Baldwin College President George P. Donaldson, affectionately known as "Dr. Pete." He was someone I admired as a child and emulated as an adult. The college was two blocks from our home and my father started taking me to its basketball games when I was in the third grade. The gym was packed with students and townspeople, and to be there as a kid was the biggest, loudest, most exciting thing imaginable. The atmosphere was electric. Whenever there was a critical point in the game, when the Abraham Baldwin team might be losing or just barely ahead, Dr. Pete would step onto the court during a timeout. He'd raise both arms, shake his fists in the air, stomp his feet, and hoot and holler to fire up the crowd.

Years later, when I was a college president myself, I did the same thing at basketball games. I have always loved taking part in student activities—and make no mistake, students know whether you are present or not. At Virginia Wesleyan, we were in a close game against Hampden-Sydney College. With seconds to go before the final buzzer, I sprinted to the student section during a timeout and began jumping up and down and acting like a total idiot. I enjoyed watching the look on the students' faces. Many, no doubt, thought, "What on earth is this grown man doing?"

"Give me a 'V'," I shouted. "Give me a 'W!' Give me a 'C!' What do you have?"

"VWC!" they shouted back.

We won the game by a single point.

As a boy, I understandably knew extraordinarily little about what college presidents did, or what their responsibilities were. I had no idea that Dr. Pete dealt with the faculty and things like budgets and strategic planning. It just seemed to me that he was a man who had a fun job and connected beautifully with his students. I liked that. I still do.

Among my life's lessons: Learn from the people around you. Think about the family, friends, and colleagues you most admire: those who encouraged and motivated you, those who had a sense of humor, and those with whom you could speak openly without being intimidated. They believed in you and you in them. Leadership is all about learning.

3

Sowing Seeds for the Ministry

My family rarely skipped a Sunday church service and like a lot of Southerners, church was central to our lives. I started thinking about a career in the ministry when I was in my teens. There was no bolt of lightning, no divine intervention, no hot summer night tent revival calling me and my friends to repent and be saved. It just seemed like a cool thing to do.

As long as I can remember, the ministry was tugging at me. Sometimes on a rainy day when I was 9 or 10 years old, my sister, Linda, and I played church. I would preach the sermon and Linda would take up the offering. That was the first inkling of my future.

My family had always befriended the pastor's family and some of their children were among my best friends. The Tifton United Methodist Church ministers were genteel, highly educated men who preached a gospel of social justice. They also were deeply involved in their community. Pastor John Wilson often officiated at Tift County High football games on Friday nights. Sammy Clark, another clergyman, found himself at the center of the civil rights movement in South Georgia and was an inspiration for me when, years later, I looked back on the segregated south of my childhood with revulsion. When I was 15 years old and in the 10th grade, Pastor George Zorn, whose son was my good buddy told me, "Billy, you have a good brain. Use it. Don't just try to get by on your personality."

While many of my high school teachers encouraged me to enroll in Sewanee—The University of the South, my father thought one college was as good as any other. "I can afford the college down the street," he'd say. In 1960 I started classes at Tifton's Abraham Baldwin Agricultural College, a branch of the University System of Georgia. Much of my time was spent playing basketball on the college's Golden Stallions team, which was average at best.

Abraham Baldwin distinguished himself as a "Founding Father" of our nation by being one of the drafters of the Constitution. He was one of two Georgia signers of the document.

Today, the college's School of Agriculture and Natural Resources is its largest area of study. The college even has a 95-acre outdoor Georgia Museum of Agriculture and Historic Village featuring restored or preserved buildings from the 1800s and early 1900s, including a doctor's office and barber shop. There's even a "Moonshine Shack." There may be a few stills left, but when I grew up life in Tifton was simple. In fact, it felt a little too simple and sheltered. I knew sticking around until corn was high on the fourth of July was not for me.

After two years at Abraham Baldwin, I enrolled at Valdosta State, one of four comprehensive universities in Georgia and one of the state's two regional universities. Though less than 50 miles south of Tifton, the school felt like a world away with its Mission Revival architecture, palm-lined walkways, and the Camellia Trail—a 3,300-foot path winding through towering pines, lined by 1,100 fragrant camellias with their stunning blooms.

At Valdosta State, a career in environmental sciences seemed like a good idea. I was majoring in biology and also thought about combining biology with law school. Still, theology and ministry continued to haunt me. I became much more socially active and was elected president of the Student Government Association. While offered a partial basketball scholarship, I quickly realized I could not study, play basketball, and be an effective student government president. It was time to grow up. It was time to make some tough choices. It also was time to hear new ideas.

One afternoon in my junior year, I found a note slid under my dormitory door from the Rev. Dr. Tom Whiting inviting me to stop by his office. He was a Yale Divinity School graduate and senior minister at the First Methodist Church in Valdosta where I regularly attended. When I met with him, he said he'd like me to be the church's youth director that summer. I had known some of the other youth directors, and they had all been theology school students. My haphazard plan had shifted to apply to medical or dental school, not enter the ministry. I told Rev. Whiting as much. "Billy," he said, "that does not matter to me. I just want you."

Well, I thought, I have to have a summer job and it's not a bad assignment to be around all these energetic and creative young people. Church member Mrs. McKey offered a room in her beautiful antebellum home with wraparound porches and magnolia trees so big you couldn't see the house from the street. I accepted the job offer and organized softball games, concerts, work projects at low-income housing, trips to youth camps at St. Simons Island, and trips to the beach and parks. I set up programs for worship services and church suppers and developed plans for tutoring small children. In other words, my main role was acting as a sort of Pied Piper for the church's young people while working with senior minister Dr. Whiting and his successor, Dr. A. Jason Shirah, and his wife, Jane. That summer I also met Fann Dewar, the woman who would become the love of my life and my wife. Her family were long-time members of Valdosta's First Methodist Church. The timing seemed perfect. Fann was a student at the all-women Wesleyan College in Macon, Georgia. I graduated from Valdosta State in December 1964.

Those few months as a youth director were the first real steps toward the ministry. After finally deciding on a career path, I began classes at Emory University's Chandler School of Theology, one of 13 seminaries affiliated with the United Methodist Church. Little did I know how life-changing those days would be.

In the summer of 1964, the South Georgia Conference of the Methodist Church hired me to join a four-person "Seminary Team," that would serve as camp counselors at Epworth-by-the-Sea's beautiful 83-acre conference and retreat center on the banks of the Frederica River below Gascoigne Bluff on St. Simons Island. Not only did Seminary Team students provide leadership for the extensive summer camps at Epworth, but they also traveled and led youth activities and Vacation Bible schools throughout the South Georgia Conference.

One Friday morning the phone rang in the Epworth-by-the-Sea office and I happened to be the one who answered it. The pastor of a church in nearby Brunswick said he was looking for someone to stand in for him on Sunday. He didn't know me and I didn't know him, but he wanted someone to lead the worship service. I said I'd be honored and would bring a group of friends and co-workers with me.

I arrived at the church early and was glad I did. Before the service, I met with the minister in his study. He told me he'd gotten word that a Black family in the area was going to integrate the church that day and there might be some kind of disturbance. At the time, that was a pretty big deal to White Southerners; Georgia was in the grips of racism. Of course, by then I had realized why he didn't want to be the one preaching that Sunday.

As I stood to read the scripture lesson during the service, a handsome Black couple and their little girl, who was about 7 years old, walked into the church and stood at the back.

"Come on in," I said enthusiastically. "We're glad to have you and we have a seat here in front if you'd like." They tentatively walked down the center aisle and sat in the same section with 25 of my friends from camp who had saved seats for them. Parishioners looked like deer in highlights, but no one got up and stomped off. The Black family was quiet and reverent. The father looked straight ahead and I felt his apprehension. After church, my friends surrounded them and eagerly shook their hands. I came down from the pulpit area and met them. We learned that the church was in their neighborhood and that they were Methodists. While some in the congregation left quickly, others saw my friends greeting the family and did the same. A few said, "Please come back again." I don't know if they ever did.

I later learned I had been painted with a broad brush, as the locals would say, for integrating their church. Well, so what? Some of us were trying to move the church into the twentieth century.

Back at seminary, I couldn't get Fann out of my mind and I knew she was going to be an important part of my life. We had our first date on my 21st birthday. I was driving an old, rusty, four-door black Mercury. It was a piece of junk by any standard. Her other dates drove new, sleek cars. I figured she would go out with me once and then go back to men with shiny cars. However, as we continued to date, Fann would say, "You left the keys in the ignition." With a straight face I'd reply, "I hope someone steals it."

When we started dating, Fann was a rising sophomore at Wesleyan College. Founded in 1836, Wesleyan carries the noble distinction of being the first college in the world chartered to grant degrees to women. Fann was beautiful. I loved her personality. She was smart and had a lot of confidence. She had a maturity about her that I liked. She seemed level-headed and focused. Before long, I realized there was no question—I wanted to marry Fann Dewar and felt obliged to ask her father for his permission.

Robert Dewar was an attorney, but while the law was his vocation, bees were his hobby and avocation. At one point, he had 500 bee hives and a staff to successfully harvest and sell his mild Gallberry honey in grocery stores across Georgia and Northern Florida. An environmentalist, he was fascinated by those thousands of buzzing pollinators. Not Fann. She helped her father pack the honey during summer vacations, but never got used to being on the receiving end of painful stings.

Fann and I already had talked about getting married so it was no surprise to her that I was going to see her father.

I made an appointment at his downtown office, sat nervously in a straight-back chair across from his desk, and asked for his blessing.

"Well, do you love her?" he asked.

I took a deep breath. "Yes sir, I surely do."

"OK," he said sternly, "but you have to promise me that you will see to it that she completes her college education."

I assured her father that she would graduate. Fann wanted to finish college (and would eventually earn a Master of Divinity, and a PhD in clinical psychology), but neither of us wanted to wait to get married.

I was studying theology, but before we wed I again kept toying with career paths. Perhaps I could be an orthodontist? While the field was lucrative, my heart was not in it and I realized the goal of making money was a shallow way to look at my lifelong profession. I wasn't certain about the ministry, either, but I was sure enough to take a closer look. Was I called to the ministry? I didn't know, but something was pulling at me and I needed to pay attention. The sense of mission seemed to compel me toward the parish.

Fann and I were married on June 5, 1965. I was 22 years old and Fann was 20. The formal, white-tie wedding was on a Saturday night at Valdosta's First Methodist Church (now First United Methodist Church) where Fann had worshipped with her family. Her eight bridesmaids were dressed in silk gowns and my eight ushers wore tuxedos. My longtime friend Jason Shirah performed our ceremony. The church was lighted with more than 100 white beeswax candles. The reception was in the church social hall.

We were flooded with beautiful wedding gifts that doubled as our sole possessions. My father, who worked for a large oil company, gave us a gasoline credit card knowing I couldn't purchase anything with it but fuel for our car. I had been enrolled in seminary for 6 months and as married students, we were poor as church mice. That credit card was a big deal.

I had a job as youth director at the Druid Hills Methodist Church. Fann got a job working at the former Davidson School for Speech Correction, near Emory.

Druid Hills was a beautiful old church on the corner of Ponce de Leon Avenue and Briarcliff Road in a section of Atlanta with stately homes and a park designed by landscape architect Frederick Law Olmsted, who co-designed New York's Central Park. It's also the neighborhood where the movie *Driving Miss Daisy* was filmed. Alas, the magnificent 70-year-old, three-story sanctuary that once was home to 3,000 parishioners is now condos. The congregation had shrunk to fewer than 100 and the church was sold in 2017. As one reporter noted, "the church's remaining congregation merged with Candler Park's Neighborhood Church (formerly Epworth Methodist) taking the cross atop the steeple with them."

My job came with an apartment in what had once been the carriage house for the elegant home in front of it. The church had an active youth ministry at the time with a gymnasium that adjoined the carriage house apartment where we lived. What a delight to be required to play basketball for my job. I was in heaven! And to live in a gym! We were young, but more than 57 years later we're living proof that you can know nothing and still come out on the other side in good shape. It didn't just happen, though—we've worked hard at our marriage and always stirred what we had.

4

Bonnie Scotland

After a year at Emory, Fann and I began talking about moving to the Northeast. Even though this country kid was intimidated by the notion of transferring to a seminary in the big leagues, I longed for more intellectual stimulation. I also knew that moving would distance me from the antediluvian south with its painful history of oppression.

I was drawn to both the School of Divinity at Yale and Drew University's Theological School. While Yale had the name recognition, Drew was breaking new ground theologically and had brought together a faculty of prolific professors who were writing books that students were studying in other seminaries around the world. Drew won out, and Fann and I moved to Madison, New Jersey, and lived in married student housing.

Drew, founded in 1867 to educate Methodist Episcopal Church ministers, reminded us of Great Britain, with stunning buildings set amidst 186 acres of hardwoods whose leaves turned crimson and gold in autumn. The "University in the Forest" was ideal for introspection. The serene campus, which adjoined the Dodge Estate, provided a peaceful space for pondering obscure biblical passages and wading through weighty tomes. Even more importantly, the faculty at Drew was exceptional. Professor Carl Michalson was internationally renowned as an intellectual and theologian; he wrote or edited six books in 7 years before dying in a plane crash in 1965. They were books that I had read at Emory and that had been praised for bringing modern psychological knowledge to classic theological problems.

Studying in an incredibly rich environment of world-class scholars gave this rural Southern boy confidence, yet I was under no delusion that I had nothing more to learn. I received a Master of Divinity degree from Drew in 1967, but I didn't want to stop studying. I was hungry for more and knew of a man considered to be one of the most renowned New Testament scholars in the English-speaking world: Dr. William Barclay, who was teaching at the University of Glasgow's Trinity College in Scotland. Anyone who has ever been in a Sunday School class in any Protestant denomination has heard or read William Barclay's words, even if they don't know his name. Barclay wrote more than 70 books, including *The Daily Study Bible*, and was a popular broadcaster on television and radio in Great Britain.

The Scottish native was a pacifist who described himself as a "liberal evangelical" who believed in universal salvation and evolution. "Jesus is the end and climax of the evolutionary process because in Him men met God," he wrote (Barclay, 1975a, p. 140). "The danger of the Christian faith is that we set up Jesus as a kind of secondary God. The Bible never, as it were, makes a second God of Jesus. Rather, it stresses the utter dependence of Jesus on God" (Barclay, 1975b, p. 188). His goal as a professor was to make the best biblical scholarship available to the average layperson and student.

Barclay was controversial, but theologians are supposed to push the envelope. Historically, theologians were the scientists of the church. Agree with him or not, he loved to make people think and stimulate a discussion. He often opened the door to his home to students and the community for ongoing discussions. Barclay was deeply loved by the British people.

Even though the likelihood of working with him was slim, I thought, "Why not give it a shot?" I wrote asking if he would consider allowing me to be his post-graduate research assistant for a year. To my delight, he said he would take me on if the University of Glasgow accepted me. It did. What an amazing opportunity—and all I had done was write him a letter. It was that simple.

Fann and I sailed across the Atlantic on the North German ocean liner SS Bremen. What an adventure we had, being immersed in another culture while crossing the ocean! Travel in itself was enriching and educational. We were kids from wee cities in Georgia who were privileged to travel to

Europe and live and study at the fourth-oldest university in the English-speaking world. The University of Glasgow's beginnings date to 1451, more than a century before the beheading of Mary Queen of Scots and before the Protestant Reformation. The university is magical, with magnificent views of steeples, domes, and spires. We strolled under the marble arches of the cloisters and through the university's sun-and-rain-drenched quadrangles, where generations of brilliant minds long before us had tread.

Dr. Barclay and I studied the parables of Jesus together, translating biblical passages from Koine, the original common Greek language of the New Testament. He'd sit on one side of his desk and I'd pull up a chair on the other side. Barclay was a small man with a receding hairline; he was almost 60 but looked much older. Stocky, he reminded me of the Pillsbury Doughboy. "I know I don't look like it now but I was Britain's fastest sprinter when I was at university," he told me.

I met with him three days a week for about an hour each meeting. He'd say, "I want you to read this chapter in the New Testament, and let's talk about it today." He smoked like a chimney, prying each unfiltered cigarette with stained fingers from a fancy gold case that he left open next to his books and fountain pen. A non-smoker, I could see his eyes when the haze cleared between puffs. I enjoyed that time with him, but I don't know what it did to my lungs.

Fann and I were living a romantic fantasy in a foreign country. Scotland in the winter is gray, damp, and cold to the bone. With no student housing, we searched for an apartment and found a third-floor walk-up near campus in a beautiful sandstone mansion house that was past its prime. We could see the remnants of an iron railing around the garden that had been chopped up for use in making ammunition in World War II.

There were no other tenants and we had the entire floor to ourselves. The house was on a campus bus line or an easy walk to the university. As an added bonus, we were living by Byres Road, one of the best shopping areas in all of Glasgow with the best bakeries. Our landlady was Polish and had outrun Hitler during World War II. She was nice but not terribly talkative or social. She advised us that we'd need "a lot of shillings" because we'd have to put a handful of shillings into the coin slots for the fireplace heaters to come to life. And in no uncertain terms, she added, "You need to know you'll have hot water for 30 minutes in the morning and 30 minutes at night."

"Do you mind giving a tip on when that is?" I asked.

"It will be the same time every day," she replied curtly and ended the conversation.

We finally figured it out. We could turn the water on at about 8:00 a.m. and 5:30 p.m. and if it felt warm, we knew we would soon have hot water. Planning dishwashing and bathing around two 30-minute hot water windows was challenging. Quite by accident, I found hot water any time I wanted. One day I walked over to the university's gym, picked up a basketball, and started shooting hoops. Another student came up to me and asked if I would like to be on the university's team. Hmm, I thought. The gym had showers with hot water and as a team member, I could take a hot shower anytime I wanted. I jokingly tell people I signed up so I could get a shower.

Rugby, football (aka soccer), and cricket were big in Britain, but basketball not so much. I was the only American on the team, along with several Russians who were studying shipbuilding, two or three Japanese students, and a Scot. By contrast, Americans made up the University of Edinburgh's team. We played all over Great Britain in our silver and blue uniforms. It was a boon to our budget because as a foreigner Fann was invited to travel by train with the team at the University's expense to all our games in St. Andrews, Cambridge, Oxford, and the University of Edinburgh. Our Glasgow players were good. Toward the end of the season, an all-star team for Scotland was chosen from players on St. Andrews, Edinburgh, and Glasgow's teams. I was chosen to be a forward. We played in the British Universities' tournament in Birmingham, England, with teams from England, Scotland, and Wales.

Though the game was familiar, the rules and language were new to me. Back home, fouls in basketball are just part of the game. Every player has five fouls, and good players want to make sure their fouls count. But in Britain at that time fouls were considered unsportsmanlike. If there was a foul, teammates might shout, "That was a bloody thing for him to do!" Back then "bloody" was considered profanity. I'm not naïve and I generally knew what the expression meant but I thought it was humorous when they'd apologize to me.

One day my friend Jim Zimmerman, in his thick Scottish brogue, confided that the University was getting ready to give me a big award. "Don't turn it down," he said. "It's a big deal over here." Not long after, he and other excited team members arrived at our flat with the big news. I was the only one selected that year to receive the Full Blue Colors, the highest honor given to athletes in the university system. The award was a necktie only honorees were allowed to wear. For years it has been framed and hanging on my office wall.

Fann also studied at the University of Glasgow and in 1969 had enough credits to complete her final semester. She graduated from Wesleyan College with a bachelor's degree in religious studies and early childhood education. Talk about stirring what you got!

Near the end of our year in Scotland, William Barclay paid me a backhanded compliment. He told me that he never knew what "you Americans" were going to be like before coming to study with him. He said on paper they all sounded like the Apostle Paul but didn't live up to that billing once he got to know them. Apparently, I was the exception—Barclay asked me to stay on for my PhD.

I was honored but we planned to be in Scotland for a year and I had committed to taking an appointment in the South Georgia Conference in June—my first church as a pastor. Barclay knocked down each of my reasons for leaving Glasgow. He had found a job for me that provided housing, and told me to go back home for a visit and return to the university the following autumn. In one of the pages of Barclay's *The Plain Man's Book of Prayers*, he assures us "... never to be afraid to follow where Thy Spirit leads" (Barclay, 1959/1987, p. 102). At the time, Fann and I felt we were being led back to Georgia and we returned home. While amazing opportunities have come my way over the years, that's one I regret not taking; it was one of the great blunders of my life. I should have returned to Scotland for my PhD with Barclay. I sometimes wonder how life would have been different had that path been taken.

On the other side of the Atlantic, change was happening within the Methodist Church. In April 1968, The Evangelical United Brethren Church and The Methodist Church united to form a new denomination, The United Methodist Church. Bishop Reuben H. Mueller, representing The Evangelical United Brethren Church, and Bishop Lloyd C. Wicke of The Methodist Church, joined hands at the constituting General Conference in Dallas, Texas. With the words, "Lord of the Church, we are united in Thee, in Thy Church and now in The United Methodist Church," the new denomination was born of two churches that had distinguished histories and influential international ministries.

Two months later, I received my appointment as a pastor assigned to Georgia's new Centerville United Methodist Church, my first church and one that would test my morals and values to the core. As the name suggests, Centerville is smack in the middle of the state. It's a bedroom community on the outskirts of Macon and adjacent to Robins Air Force Base, the largest industrial complex in Georgia and host to Warner Robins Air Logistics Center and the 78th Air Base Wing.

In many ways, Centerville was part of the old South. Fann and I had looked at life from both sides now. Our spirit and outlook were aligned with a new generation who saw the world differently.

5

Bridging a Racial and Cultural Divide

In April 1968, a few days after the assassination of Martin Luther King, Jr., Fann and I traveled to Coventry, England, to visit the 14th-century St. Michael's Cathedral. Known colloquially as Coventry Cathedral, the Gothic church was destroyed in a nighttime blitz on November 14, 1940, by the German Luftwaffe as part of its "Moonlight Sonata" operation. More than 500 military combat aircraft dropped 36,000 incendiary bombs on the city of Coventry that day, killing hundreds, destroying thousands of homes, and gutting most of the city's structures. Only the church's tower, spire, and the bronze effigy and tomb of its first bishop survived. As a symbol of reconciliation, a new cathedral was constructed alongside the bombed-out ruins in the 1950s and dedicated in 1962.

Fann and I were walking along the perimeter of the church's war-torn skeletal remains when we heard a magnificent bass voice in the new cathedral singing the much loved century-old African American spiritual "Swing Low, Sweet Chariot." We quietly went inside and listened to a memorial service rehearsal for the slain American civil rights leader. We had been horrified days earlier as we watched the news and read reports of King's death, yet to hear the gorgeous spiritual being sung moved us to the core. Here we were, thousands of miles away from our Georgia home at such a historic place with no one we knew, yet we shared the universal loss. We stood there and listened, tears flooding our eyes.

King had been killed on April 4 by a bullet to his head, a day after his famous "I See the Promised Land" speech. He was buried 5 days later in Atlanta as hundreds of thousands of people clogged streets and sidewalks to get a glimpse of his casket pulled by a creaking, mule-drawn wooden wagon. Inside Ebenezer Baptist Church was "the greatest galaxy of prominent national figures there had ever been in Atlanta," a local television station reported, "among them Robert Kennedy, George Romney, Jacqueline Kennedy, Richard Nixon, Nelson Rockefeller, Hubert Humphrey, Harry Belafonte, Wilt Chamberlain, and James Brown."

Violence followed. For days after King's assassination, activists rioted in more than 100 American cities. Protestors were savagely beaten. Thirty-nine people died and thousands were injured or arrested. Fann and I had spent a lovely year in the "Dear Green Place," as Glasgow is known, and were coming back to a country defined not by spring's soothing pastel palette of lustrous greens, pinks, and yellows, but by stark blacks, whites, and reds of a racist nation torn and bleeding.

King's death sparked social unrest that had been simmering with decades of overt racial discrimination, poverty, and police brutality as Blacks justifiably demanded the right to vote, attend public schools, drink from the same water fountains, use the same restrooms, walk through the same front doors of restaurants, movie theaters, and hotels, and sit at the same lunch counters as White people. Millions of Black folks had fled the South's racial caste system, only to be met with much of the same segregation, discrimination, and violence in the North.

In 1961, 7 years before King's death, Georgia civil rights activist John Lewis—later to serve in Congress for more than 30 years—and 11 other so-called Freedom Riders stopped in Rock Hill, South Carolina, on their way to Louisiana to test a Supreme Court ruling that made segregation in interstate transportation illegal. Lewis was savagely beaten by a member of the Ku Klux Klan after trying to enter the waiting room marked "Whites" at a Greyhound bus station.

In the South, Alabama Governor George Wallace was the poster boy for racism, in 1963 declaring in his January, 1963, inaugural address, "... segregation now, segregation tomorrow, segregation forever." In 1964, President Lyndon B. Johnson stepped in, signing into law the Civil Rights Act. It prohibited discrimination in public places, integrated schools and other public facilities, and made employment discrimination illegal. It was the most sweeping civil rights legislation since Reconstruction but it didn't seem to matter. White Southerners did everything they could to prevent Black Southerners from voting, not unlike today.

In February 1965, unarmed Black activist Jimmie Lee Jackson was beaten and shot by state troopers while participating in a peaceful voting rights march in Marion, Alabama. He was 26 years old. Jackson was laid to rest in an old slave burial ground. His headstone has since been vandalized, bearing the marks of at least one shotgun blast.

In response to Jackson's death, on March 7, 1965, civil rights warrior Hosea Williams helped coordinate a 54-mile march from Selma to Montgomery, Alabama. Police tore into protesters with tear gas, billy clubs, and whips as protestors tried to walk across the Edmund Pettus Bridge over the Alabama River en route to Montgomery. "Bloody Sunday" galvanized Congress and on August 5, 1965, legislators passed the Voting Rights Act. President Lyndon B. Johnson signed it into law the next day. Literacy tests and other roadblocks that prevented Black citizens from voting were prohibited. This "act to enforce the 15th amendment to the Constitution" became law 95 years after the amendment was ratified. Today, voting rights again are being eroded by racist legislators, state by state.

The South continued to seethe in a desperate attempt to keep Jim Crow laws in place. Little had changed in my home state of Georgia, where angry White people continued to use brute force to jail men, women, and children because of the color of their skin. And here I was, a 26-year-old privileged White man of the cloth with my first parish in Centerville. I was the same age Jimmie Lee Jackson had been when he was killed.

The Centerville United Methodist Church was small. It helped that the congregation was young; I played football with the teenagers and the kids liked me. It was a different story with some of their parents. While Fann and I lived in the parsonage across the street from the church, we were politically miles apart from many of our church members. Centerville is about 20 miles south of Macon. It didn't offer much in the way of intellectual stimulation and there weren't many people who shared our views that segregation was not only inappropriate but morally unjustified.

In Georgia, law enforcement officers were putting Blacks behind bars just because they were Black. I was passionate about trying to bridge the racial and cultural divide that was so pervasive in the South and brought that belief into many of my sermons. Some parishioners scolded me, not-so-subtly lecturing me that I shouldn't talk about anything that had to do with racism or quote Martin Luther King. Still, a few did pull me aside to say, "We needed to hear that" and thanked me, but those comments were the exception.

Shortly after arriving in Centerville, a Lutheran minister friend told me that Selma march protester Hosea Williams had been jailed in Perry, 30 miles from Macon in the heart of Georgia. Williams was born in Attapulgus, Georgia, the son of blind parents. For almost a half-century he protested racial discrimination at some of the most dangerous confrontations of the Civil Rights Movement. Williams joined the National Association for the Advancement of Colored People (NAACP) after being beaten for drinking from a "Whites Only" water fountain in Americus, Georgia. A staff sergeant in an all-Black unit during World War II, Williams was the only member of his unit to survive a Nazi bombing. He spent a year in a European hospital before returning to the United States with a Purple Heart. He earned a bachelor's degree in chemistry from Morris Brown College, a master's degree from Atlanta University, and was the first African-American research chemist hired by the federal government in the Deep South.

Now he was behind bars in Perry, Georgia.

"Let's see if we can find him and get him out of jail," my friend said. Little did we know what we were stepping into.

During the 20-minute drive, I said to my friend, "Let me talk because with my drawl they'll clearly know I'm a Southerner;" my friend was from the North. We parked the car and walked toward the courthouse. A man wearing overalls smiled and bid us good morning as we passed him on the sidewalk in the courthouse square. We returned his greeting. We had no reason to feel unsafe; we were White and we were ministers. We walked into the sheriff's office where there were three or four deputies and the same number of secretaries. Everyone greeted us politely as we entered the office.

In my best authoritative voice, I announced, "We're looking for a civil rights leader named Hosea Williams." You could have heard a pin drop. Their affable facial expressions changed and they glared at me with utter disdain. A snarling deputy snapped, "We don't know where any Hosea Williams is but we know where a goddamned nigger named Williams is. Get out." We hadn't expected such hostility and all of a sudden we felt our lives were being threatened. Frightened, we did as we were told. As we hightailed it toward my car, we looked back and saw a couple of the hefty deputy sheriffs watching us from the courthouse steps. The guy we had seen earlier, the one wearing overalls who had greeted us so cordially, was standing on the sidewalk near the front of the building.

"Are these guys causing you trouble?" he hollered to the deputies. Before they could answer, he shoved my friend to the ground, breaking his glasses.

I helped him up and we dashed to the car. I figured the only reason the guy hadn't gone after me was that at more than six-foot, three inches, I was taller. We drove away, shaking. We could hardly speak. Could people really hate someone this much because of the color of their skin?

We later learned that Hosea Williams eventually was released from jail. He had been in Perry joining other civil rights activists who demanded equal treatment by holding nonviolent sit-ins and by blocking the front of Perry's drugstores, grocery stores, and other businesses. Black folks were trying to shut the town down and they were doing a pretty good job of it—until law enforcement started arresting them. After every jail in Houston (pronounced House-tin) County was full, hundreds of Black folks and a few White folks were loaded onto school buses and taken outside of town, where they were herded like cattle into a huge fenced-in open area. I later heard the only running water was from a hose. A few large hardwood trees provided scant shade. Maybe there was a single portable outhouse but there wasn't much else. It was bleak. I don't know how long the protesters were kept in those conditions but at some point the National Guard and state troopers were called in to liberate them.

When I was growing up, my family believed in integration, even though Tifton was no different from other segregated cities and towns. One evening my father announced that he was going to a meeting at our church where a vote would be taken allowing African-Americans to sit with White folks during Sunday services. This was a big deal in the 1950s and 1960s in the South. No Blacks had asked to join our Methodist church but a lot of its White members were petrified that they might. Not Big Bill. "The only Christian thing to do is invite anyone coming for worship to be seated," he said as he left the house. The meeting was long. It was a school night, but my mother let my sister and me stay up late. We waited impatiently for hours to hear how the congregation had voted

"The vote was close, but it passed," my father announced when he returned home, worn out but pleased with the decision he had championed. Then he grew somber. "I lost my best customer tonight."

The owner of one of the largest trucking lines in the South had pulled my father aside at the church meeting. "Bill," he said, "if you feel that way about integrating the church, then I'll need to take my business somewhere else."

That night my Dad was the most courageous man in the world. The threat didn't change his mind or his vote. He did lose the trucking company's business but he made sure I knew that taking a stand was more important than losing his premier customer. He sat on the corner of my bed and told me, "Always do the right thing, and remember that right is right even if no one is doing it and wrong is wrong even if everyone is doing it."

I am not going to suggest I have always followed through on this principle, but I have always tried to let it guide me. Once we were traveling to a meeting and on a flat stretch of road between Columbus and Macon when some distance ahead we saw a pickup truck trying to pass a huge dump truck. The dump truck blasted into that pickup like it was in slow motion. We witnessed the driver of the pickup sail through his side window, landing in a ditch. We drove to the wreck, jumped out of the car, and went to see if we could help the injured driver who was groaning in pain. A farmer who had been sitting on his porch at a nearby house came running. This was before cell phones so I asked the farmer if I could use his house phone to call an ambulance.

The person who answered the phone paused. "Is he Black or White?"

"I don't know but his blood is red," I replied.

That story has stayed with me. The young man—who was Black—went to a Macon hospital and survived. That kind of question is what a lot of people asked in the Deep South and one I did my darndest to show through my words and deeds that we are all alike, no matter the color of our skin.

That value is something I have tried to instill in my sons, too. Many years later, while I was the president at Brevard College, our middle son, Robert, played basketball on the First United Methodist Church team, which I coached. It was one of 15 teams in a league representing local Methodist, Episcopal, Presbyterian, Baptist, Catholic, and Lutheran churches.

My sons asked if I knew why there was not a team in the church league with a Black player. I thought they were kidding at first. I told my boys to invite some of their Black friends to play on our team. "Tell them we'd very much like to have them join us."

I had four Black guys and one of my sons in the starting lineup for our Saturday morning games. We beat everybody; all these kids were so good they could've been on the local high school's team. But you would not believe the hostility from the coaches at other local churches.

"You know all the players on our teams are members of our churches?" they'd reprimand me, not-so-subtly referring to their all-White teams.

Nowhere did the league bylaws say players were required to belong to a church. With me as president of Brevard College and our three sons all popular in school, we were the right bunch to integrate the league. And wouldn't you know, we won the league championship.

I have tried to do the right thing and stand by my values. It hasn't been always easy, but I relied on my father's advice: do what is right, not what is expedient.

Those whom I have held in the highest esteem taught me the most valuable lessons of my life. Although my courage has at times escaped me, the values remain: Stand up. Speak up. When witnessing racism, fraud, abuse, repression, or any other injustice, call out the perpetrators and demand action.

6

For Everything a Season

After a Sunday worship service in Centerville, one of the most prominent members of the church angrily pointed his finger at me. "Preacher," he said, "if you are not for George Wallace, you should be shot." Those were not the kind of people I wanted to be around. After two years, I got tired of fighting wrenching battles. It was high time to move on to another parish.

United Methodist Church clergy typically are appointed by the bishop and Conference of Superintendents, not called or hired, with the idea of matching the "gifts and graces" of each pastor or deacon with the ministry needs of a congregation. But Jason Shirah, the friend who married Fann and me, was the senior pastor at St. Luke United Methodist Church in Columbus, Georgia, and asked me to join him as his associate pastor.

Even though the Centerville church had not been a good fit, I felt I should stick it out longer. That changed after Jason and his wife, Jane, invited Fann and me to visit them in Columbus. After dinner, they took us downtown to see St. Luke, one of the largest churches in Georgia. Even today, parishioners are from families who have been St. Luke members for generations. They are leaders not only in Columbus but statewide and nationally.

The church, rebuilt in 1948 after a fire, is an impressive Georgian brick structure with a portico supported by four towering white columns and a white steeple and spire topped by a cross. Eight stained glass windows in the sanctuary depict events from the creation to the establishment of the Methodist Church in America. Jason unlocked the front door and slowly began to turn on the interior lights, revealing the magnificence of a church that could seat 700 worshipers. I was overwhelmed and I could envision a bigger world with a greater sense of mission and more opportunities. We were ready to leave Centerville. In June 1970, we moved to Columbus, Georgia, where I became associate pastor and minister of youth at St. Luke UMC. I accepted Jason's job offer for only one year because I still was thinking about going back to Scotland for further graduate study. Life had different plans.

The 1970s were exciting years for us. Fann and I were young. We had become the parents of three sons: William Thomas III was born June 11, 1971; Robert Dewar was born February 15, 1974 (a day-late Valentine's gift); and David Benjamin came into our lives on December 15, 1976. By the end of the decade, I would have served as pastor of four churches, uprooting our family four times. I was continuing my education and we had a growing circle of friends, most who had children our children's ages. The Vietnam War ended, President Nixon resigned in disgrace following the Watergate break-in, Americans were taken hostage in Iran, Elvis Presley died, the Supreme Court made abortion legal, Jimmy Carter was elected president, and Apple and Microsoft were launched.

We were happy where we were. My one-year commitment at St. Luke turned into four, and we met and became close friends with many inspiring and highly motivated people of all ages, socio-economic levels, and professions. They were community and state leaders, and philanthropists—people of depth and substance Fann and I had longed for and who taught us lessons by the examples of their lives and choices. From parishioner Betty B. Woolbright it was a lesson about grace. She was one of the most compassionate people I've ever known. Affectionately called Bebe, she had two daughters in the St. Luke Youth Group, Laura and Martha, and was a social worker by training. She was non-judgmental, a quality adults love and young people crave. She taught me many things. Not judging was near the top of the list—a trait I struggle with constantly. Also among her many outstanding qualities was her ability to focus on the "now" and not allow anxiety-producing possibilities to crowd the picture. One time we were boarding a 747 airliner to Europe with 30 young people and 10 adults. Betty told one anxious child, "Honey, this thing is so big they won't even show it all to us at one time."

Bill Turner also was a tireless example of servant leadership whose influence on me continues to this day. He was a giant of a man from whom I learned a great deal about dedication, servanthood, commitment, accessibility, and philanthropy. For 60 years William Bradley Turner taught the high school Sunday School classes at St. Luke. Turner, who died in 2017 at the age of 94, was one of the wealthiest men in the country. His grandfather was co-chair of the Coca-Cola Company for nearly three decades. Turner—"Mr. Bill" or "BT," as he was called—was chairman of the Bradley Company, whose main product was Char-Broil, one of the first charcoal grills on the market. He also was the third generation of his family to serve on the Coca-Cola Board of Directors. He taught me that if you give others credit there is no telling how much can be accomplished.

Another friend was Hugh Landrum, who signed a franchise agreement with Midas International Corp. in 1956. Landrum's Macon auto repair shop became the nation's first Midas Muffler Shop. Yet as busy and important as Woolbright, Turner, and Landrum were, they always made time to meet with me and offer their wisdom and guidance.

Even though by then I had a Master of Divinity degree from Drew, I pined for yet more education. After 2 years at St. Luke, I again enrolled in Emory's Candler School of Theology—this time to pursue a doctorate in sacred theology. While it was a punishing 100-mile commute between Columbus and Atlanta, I could still work as St. Luke's associate pastor.

Fann had been creating innovative teaching and learning opportunities for kindergarten-age children but was forced to "retire" because she was four-and-a-half-months pregnant with our first child, William. As strange as it may seem now, in 1971 teachers were not allowed to continue teaching if they were "showing" that they were pregnant. She later found an unexpected career in television—something she had never dreamed of. The program director for the local ABC affiliate in Columbus telephoned the Muscogee County School Board office and asked if they knew anyone they could talk with about children's television programming. Unbeknownst to her, the school board recommended Fann.

Our home phone rang and a very resonant voice said, "This is Carroll Ward, program director for Channel 9. We are revamping our children's programming. You have been recommended as someone we should contact. Would you come and talk with us about your ideas?" At eight-and-a-half-months pregnant Fann met with the TV station's management, who then asked her to make an audition tape. She agreed to make the tape although she couldn't believe she would actually be offered the job. Fann was surprised they offered her the job and she accepted. For the next 3 years, she planned and hosted the children's TV show *Small World*, which aired for 30 minutes each weekday morning. She became a very popular young woman among the preschool set throughout that part of Georgia and Alabama.

One day Fann was in a local toy store looking for props for the show when she felt something on her legs. She looked down and discovered a little boy who had recognized her and was hugging her ankles. His mother, standing nearby, exclaimed "He loves you!" It was a precious and memorable moment to see how powerful a positive, educational TV show can be for a child.

This was a unique, magical time in our lives. Young people visited our home constantly and more than 100 regularly attended Sunday evening Youth Group at the church. We accompanied them on trips to Europe, California, canoeing, hiking, and camping expeditions, and to amusement parks and we worked with Open Door Community Center, led by Sybil Dodson. Teenagers came to us with all their joys and troubles, especially when they didn't know where else to turn to talk about life choices, colleges, depression, pregnancy fears, or drugs. You name it, they came. I also coached the boys' basketball team. Our son, William, was two-and-a-half years old when baby Robert Greer was born in 1974. Fann and Robert had been home from the hospital less than an hour when I went off to coach the church basketball tournament in Atlanta. Fann's mother had never said a negative word about me—at least that I know of—but that day she came to Fann and with the gravest concern asked, "He's going to Atlanta for the weekend to coach a basketball team?" The trip had been previously planned and it was fine with Fann. I wasn't gone long—and we won the championship.

Each June at the South Georgia Annual Conference the bishop announces new parish assignments. In 1974, after four years in Columbus, I was appointed pastor of the United Methodist Church in Cuthbert, Georgia, as well as the chaplain and a faculty member at two-year Andrew College in Cuthbert. I've always enjoyed working with young people and it seemed like a good fit. Church members who were at the conference came up to greet me.

The conversation went something like this, "Pleased to have you coming. Has anybody told you there are two churches?"

"No," I said. "I'm all ears."

"Well, there's also a rural church named Benevolence and you also preach there the second and fourth Sundays of each month."

Cuthbert is a small community and I could only imagine what the "rural" church was like. Although economically depressed and long past its prime, the region is proud of its agriculture, pulpwood, and timber products. It is 40 miles southwest of Albany, Georgia, 60 miles south of Columbus, and 25 miles east of the Alabama border. The more than 400-mile Chattahoochee River supplies 70% of Atlanta's drinking water. It rolls into the county's northwestern corner, then flows southward along its western boundary with Alabama. Fletcher "Smack" Henderson Jr., an influential African-American bandleader in the jazz and swing movement, grew up there. But Cuthbert is tiny and moving there was not easy for us after having lived in Columbus, Georgia's second-largest city. And I felt bad for Fann— and still do—who had a nice career at the local TV station. It did turn out to be quite an adventure and helped me decide higher education would be my next move.

The rural Benevolence wooden church, which no doubt was built more than 100 years ago, was small and picturesque and sat on the side of an old clay country road. By the time I moved to Cuthbert, there were only seven members left at Benevolence and they were set in their ways. A parishioner used his pocket knife to unlock the door. A water bucket in the center aisle caught rainwater from a leaky roof. One man sat in a back pew and one in front, where they no doubt had perched for generations. They didn't want anything to do with the church in Cuthbert. Even though Easter didn't fall on one of the regularly scheduled Sundays, I said I was willing to come out to help celebrate. They looked at each other and said, "We want to stick to our schedule." Another time I brought about 20 students to Benevolence, who cleaned and painted it inside and out. The following Sunday the seven parishioners showed up and barely noticed.

In 1977 I earned a doctorate from Emory's Candler School of Theology in sacred theology, specializing in theological ethics. I had begun the degree program while in Columbus and completed it five years later after moving to Cuthbert. Learning was my passion and by this time I had been bitten by the higher education bug. The idea of shifting careers from parish ministry to that of college administrator began brewing.

While pastor of the Cuthbert United Methodist Church I became dear friends with two successive presidents of Andrew College affiliated with the United Methodist Church. College President Jacob C. "Jake" Martinson and his successor, Walter Y. Murphy, had offered me numerous opportunities to teach courses on the Old and New Testaments, to be the college chaplain, to be a part of their administrative team, and to serve as secretary of the Board of Trustees and its Executive Board.

Both men and their families became friends and invited Fann and me to numerous events at the college. We were in and out of each other's homes regularly. When Jake Martinson's dad died, I held Jake in my arms as we both cried. Months later, Fann and I were vacationing in western North Carolina and stayed in the basement apartment of Jake Martinson's in-laws. Late one evening we heard Jake's mother-in-law screaming and sobbing. We ran upstairs to learn that their son had died in a private plane crash. These two traumatic times brought us even closer.

I am convinced Martinson and Murphy guided me toward the presidency of Andrew. Those were golden years, not brought about by my brilliant leadership, far from it. Those years came about because of our friendships. You "stir what you've got" and it happens.

My affiliation with Andrew College continued after Martinson moved on to become president of Brevard College in Brevard, North Carolina, and later to the top post at High Point College, 200 miles east of Brevard. Murphy, who succeeded Martinson as president of Andrew, continued to keep me involved with the college and also asked me to be on the Executive Committee of its Board of Trustees.

In 1979, we left Cuthbert (little did we know we'd be back) and moved to Macon, Georgia, where I was appointed pastor of Forest Hills United Methodist Church. It was a very successful, and gratifying time. Most of the parishioners were about our age and I worked mostly with couples who had small children. We had a great daycare center for preschoolers that brought many young families to the church regularly. Because the program was so popular, quite often the children's parents joined the church. Forest Hill's membership grew from 600 to 700 in one year and was recognized for being the fastest-growing United Methodist Church in Georgia.

One Sunday I invited my old friend Walter Murphy to travel from Cuthbert to preach at Forest Hills. Afterward, we went to lunch. "I need to tell you something," Murphy confided. "I am leaving Andrew to take the job as president of four-year LaGrange College," a United Methodist-affiliated school in LaGrange, Georgia, an hour southwest of Atlanta along I-85. "I think you ought to be interested in the Andrew job."

"Walter," I said, "I could be very interested in the Andrew job."

7

Andrew College

If I was going to make the change, now was the time. For years I had entertained the idea of a ministry in higher education as an administrator. My education had well prepared me for ordination in the United Methodist Church, to teach and to preach, to dip my toes in collegiate life as chaplain at Andrew College, and to serve on the executive board of the college's Board of Trustees. Becoming president of the college seemed like the next step.

I was ready to make the move from a parish to what seemed like an even larger and more compelling ministry in higher education, while aware many would not understand why I wanted to switch careers. How could a career be greater than working with young people in their daily lives while making life-shaping decisions? Many, including my own family, did not grasp the diverse calling of higher education and its ability to change lives. Working with and relating to young people were my gifts that seemed to fit with this specialized ministry. As well-meaning people lamented my "leaving the ministry" I was reminded of Nehemiah, the 7th-century BCE Hebrew prophet, a biblical character who had inspired me for years. As the story goes, he stood on a pile of rubble in the baking sun repairing the Wall of Jerusalem, which had been demolished. In ancient times few things were more important than the city wall. Since Jerusalem was his hometown it was imperative to Nehemiah that the wall be rebuilt and the city protected. Three times the city fathers pleaded with Nehemiah to come down from the pile. Three times he said, "I am doing a great work and cannot come down."

Nehemiah stands as a testament to faithfulness and perseverance. We must each seek our own "great work," one that gives us purpose and inspires us to stay the course and not come down, to continue building from the rubble despite what others say. Something is compelling about purpose without distraction, but the purpose is not always something we inherently know, and it can change over time. Though I didn't realize it right away, the clergy and academia were my vocations, and lifelong learning was a necessary and enjoyable bridge between the two. I wanted, and needed, a good education to pursue my dreams. I didn't always have a straight path along life's highways to achieve my goals; sometimes there were dead ends, sometimes unpaved side roads, but I never stopped the great work of continually learning from those around me.

In June 1980, I became president of Andrew College in Cuthbert, Georgia. Though this shift in my career was thrilling, on other levels it had its heartbreaks. Along with many notes and phone calls of congratulations from well-wishers were three letters that threatened me and my family for taking the job. Fann was terrified for us and our children. Living in Cuthbert the first time had been difficult and now we were receiving intimidating letters. Would it be possible for me to move our family with our three young sons back to a place where such hate and malice existed? It was determined the letters had originated from a deranged person who wanted the job. Yet that terrible correspondence was a reminder of how complicated my new position would be and the importance of assembling not only a strong administrative team but remaining in close contact with supportive family and friends. To complicate life even more, we had to decide what was best for our children's education. We had always been strong public school supporters but realized our children needed a stronger school system than was provided by Randolph County. After careful consideration we decided to enroll our children in The Lakeside School 35 miles away in Eufaula, Alabama.

We moved back to Cuthbert with new work to do. As pastor of Cuthbert United Methodist Church from 1974–1979, I had been heavily involved in the college and knew a lot of what the work involved, but there was much to learn. Still, I realized I was the person for the job and was eager to get going.

While an Andrew board member who attended many meetings in the president's office, my thoughts often drifted to *being* the president. With the stereotypical manners of someone from the Deep South, I never let on that I might be envious of their careers, even though part of me was so envious I could hardly stand it. I wanted very much to get my hands on Andrew and often thought there was no reason why Andrew's best days were behind it. I wanted to shout to the world "Wow, I hope to get this office someday!"

And now here I was, following in the footsteps of two men whom I greatly admired. Before sunrise on that first morning at the new job—and new career—I drove less than two blocks from the McDonald house, the official president's home, to Old Main, the college's administrative offices. The stunning five-story Victorian structure is the premier building on campus, constructed in 1892 for $25,000 after a fire had ripped through the campus. Andrew had served as a Confederate hospital during the Civil War and rightfully boasts of being the country's first college to offer physical education classes for women. Originally named Andrew Female College, in 1866 a physical education course was added to the curriculum, the first such class to be required of women in the South. The school, coed since 1956, was small, with enrollment for decades hovering around 350 students. In 2018, Andrew also offered a bachelor of science degree in business and another B.S. degree in organizational leadership.

It had been a leap of faith for me to switch careers. As chief educational and administrative officer, I was now responsible for the college's students, faculty, staff, and board of trustees, along with the supervision, management, and governance of the school. What an honor to be Andrew's president, but beneath the veneer of self-confidence was a guy who was anxious and not so sure of himself having not come up through the ranks of academia or administration. In many ways, I was starting at the top of my new field instead of climbing the traditional ladder from department head, dean, or vice president. While there were similarities between "town and gown," my biggest challenge was trying to figure out how to be a leader of an institution of higher learning versus overseeing a parish. And I needed to learn quickly. Who could I trust to lean on? Telephoning Martinson and Murphy and peppering them with queries every five minutes was out of the question. What "how to" books or manuals should I read? Who would be my muse?

I was afraid but decided fear wasn't always a bad thing. Too much fear and I'd become paralyzed and ineffective and I didn't want to feel like I was wearing a strait-jacket. Just the right amount of trepidation would keep me focused and moving in a positive direction.

Fann had been by my side as a pastor's wife at four churches. She had given up her creative job as a TV host and now was the first lady of Andrew College. Thankfully, Fann was then a stay-at-home mom who could be with the boys while I figured out my new role, but she was far more than a mother and housewife. She was my confidant and my best friend, as well as the college's full-time volunteer as event planner, horticulturist, and interior decorator, taking charge of upgrading and beautifying the Andrew campus buildings and grounds.

While we loved working for the college, Cuthbert—both the town and the college—had major challenges. Cuthbert was in the middle of nowhere and it was a deprived nowhere. When our son, Robert, broke his arm playing football, we drove 60 miles to Columbus for treatment. Andrew had almost no endowment (today its endowment is more than $10 million) and the college's facilities were sketchy with broken windows and pigeons flying through the Old Main towers. Scratching for nickels and dimes to pay the monthly light bill was a constant challenge. We had talked about those issues when I was on the Andrew board but never managed to do anything about them. Suddenly they were staring me in the face. It was my problem. I was the one who was responsible and there was no passing the buck.

I, like my peers, sought perfection, but in hindsight that was just plain stupid—perfection doesn't exist. Fortunately, the staff and faculty were wonderful and dedicated. But I knew what I didn't know, so I enrolled in Georgia State University's PhD program in higher education administration. It was a way to jump-start my new career to grasp the inner workings of budgets, human resources, legal matters, marketing, and all the other aspects of running a college. I was driven.

Getting that second doctorate wasn't easy. I thought driving 100 miles from Columbus to Atlanta for my doctorate in sacred theology from Emory was grueling. This commute was worse. While working full-time as the president of Andrew College, I'd travel two-and-a-half hours to Atlanta to attend classes and return home the same night. The chair of the Andrew College Board of Trustees, one other trustee, and Fann were the only ones who knew what I was doing. I'd get home at 1:30 a.m. or 2:00 a.m. and be at the office early the next morning for work. While learning on the job, I had to find my way and figure out what worked for me and what didn't. And I had to prove myself capable of being in charge of hundreds of people and the buildings where they worked, lived, taught, and learned. I had to assemble a support system. Failing at even the smallest tasks could result in a train wreck down the road.

At Andrew, I inherited a supportive faculty with a passion for the college and its students. They were brilliant teachers and scholars who knew I needed a great deal of help. They realized quickly I had a love for the place but almost no knowledge of how to do the job. They were mostly young and energetic and we bonded, playing many late afternoon pick-up football, volleyball, and basketball games.

To a person they were delightful. Three staff members spent one weekend programming the college's first computer so it would be up and running by the start of classes on Monday. Music instructor Larry Belt took average voices and coached them, recognizing talent in even ordinary students. He worked tirelessly to create delightful bi-annual madrigal dinners. Controller Audrey Faircloth taught me about budgets. She was a quiet, smart, and lovely lady who didn't belittle me for my lack of fiscal know-how.

That first summer at Andrew was stiflingly hot. I spent much of it literally crawling around our major classroom building installing cheap brown carpet and applying fresh paint to walls with Dean of Students Jimmy Gilbert, who also was the physical education professor; Academic Dean Charles Lynn, a math and biology professor; and Larry Brown, our information technology guru, and business professor, who earlier in his career had worked for NASA. There was no money in the budget to have someone do those jobs for us. The physical plant staff were involved in other pressing projects and while there was enough money for materials, we provided the labor. There was a job that needed to be done and we did it. College or university presidents talk about thinking strategically. There was no strategic thinking here. We just responded to a need and did the work ourselves. These guys were smart, supportive, and down-to-earth, with not a prima donna among them.

None of these folks had a self-serving agenda; they wanted us all to thrive and for the college to grow. I would not have succeeded without them and will always be indebted to the Andrew professors and instructors for teaching me how to be a college president.

Lessons learned? Passion outweighs knowledge. Always acknowledge when you've made a mistake. Don't be ashamed to say, "I don't know," "I don't understand," or "I was wrong." Then acquire the knowledge you need—always look for opportunities to educate yourself.

8

New Challenges, New Goals

After more than 5 years as president of Andrew College, my old friend Jake Martinson telephoned. He was leaving Brevard College in Brevard, North Carolina to take the reins of High Point College, now High Point University. The United Methodist Church-affiliated school is 20 minutes from Greensboro and Winston-Salem, North Carolina. And he was nominating me to replace him.

Andrew had been my first presidency. I had given myself to it completely. They needed me, or so I thought. We had worked tirelessly to improve facilities and grow the endowment. Old Main had been renovated and remodeled; the Rhodes Science Center was constructed; tennis courts were installed; the D. Abbott Turner Dining Hall was built, giving space in Old Main for a much-needed student center; the McDonald House, (the president's residence) was renovated, rewired, and redecorated; two guest rooms were added to the Reed Alumni House; and seed money given for the Jinks Gymnasium. Leaving Andrew would be walking away before the job was finished. I said no.

Weeks later Brevard Board Chair Johnie Jones, an iconic man and chief executive officer of J.A. Jones Inc. in Charlotte, North Carolina, called. Our family was vacationing at St. Simons Island, Georgia, in the days before extensive cell phone service, but somehow he had tracked me down.

"Billy, you are saying no to us but you haven't even been to see us," he purred in his smooth-talking Southern voice. He added that St. Simons was not all that far from his Charlotte office and asked Fann and me to drive over to visit him. From there, he said, we'd take a look at Brevard.

Several days later Fann and I headed to Charlotte, arriving on an early summer afternoon. Jones was a tall, distinguished-looking man with a pleasant smile and one of those unforgettable firm handshakes. He reminded me of John Wayne. On the elevator ride to his office he told us that, to our surprise, he had invited the entire search committee to meet us. "They're upstairs in our boardroom waiting on us," he said with a knowing wink.

Some two-dozen people were sitting around a table longer than any I had ever seen. As we walked in the door Johnie Jones announced, "The Greers are here." Committee members started clapping. Fann and I looked at each other. "Holy smokes," I mumbled as we were directed to two vacant chairs. Like it or not, we were being interviewed.

They were up to speed on my record at Andrew and it was clear they wanted to know us as people and if we were the right fit. As we walked out of that boardroom 2 hours later, we felt energized. Johnie Jones walked us to the elevator. "Thanks for coming," he said. "You looked good on paper but look even better in person."

My head was spinning and I desperately wanted to talk with Fann about the interview, Johnie Jones, the search committee, our children, the public schools in Brevard, and what the move would mean to our family. Sure, a search committee had unexpectedly interviewed us, but we also had to consider them. We paid careful attention in those early hours and days to what our bodies were telling us. Psychiatrists refer to people as "somatizing" a problem or issue. That is to say, we can remove stress and anxiety from our conscious mind but it comes out in other ways in our bodies through back pain, headache, stomach problems, or other issues. If the job as president of Brevard College was offered, would we really leave Andrew?

After meeting with the search committee we drove to Brevard, a small city in Transylvania County not far from Asheville, an area known for its 250 waterfalls and its white squirrels! Brevard College today offers bachelor's degrees, but at the time it was a junior college. The small, private United Methodist school, which dates to 1853, is dotted with red brick buildings on

100 rural acres nestled in the Southern Appalachian Mountains close to the Pisgah National Forest and DuPont State Forest.

The striking Brevard College Stone Fence and Gate had been built by the Works Progress Administration in 1936–1937 and was added to the National Register of Historic Places in 1993. By the end of the visit and tour, we were smitten. Neither of us hesitated long; if offered the job, we'd go.

The call came. It was Johnie Jones and this time he said he and the board wanted me to take the job. But leaving a place I'd poured my heart into was grueling. The announcement that I was leaving Andrew did not go well. The faculty and staff were angry. They felt hurt and betrayed. One professor I especially admired was Sarah Anne Staples, who taught biology. She could have taught anywhere, but she loved Andrew. She came to my office and said with so much venom, "You are not leaving even if I have to get a lawyer and sue to keep you here. You have started us down this road of success and you are not leaving." My heart ached.

Exiting Andrew was like walking away from my child. The Andrew staff, faculty, and community had taken me in and taught me so much. But I was reminded of the Kenny Rogers lyrics in the song "The Gambler."

> You've got to know when to hold 'em
> Know when to fold 'em
> Know when to walk away
> And know when to run. (Schlitz, 1978)

While the move from Andrew was excruciatingly difficult, it was time to fold 'em and discover new challenges and new horizons. I felt it all—pain, guilt, sadness. Once again I was faced with the importance and responsibility of relationships yet I felt like I was leaving Andrew in the lurch. The Andrew Board asked that I stay on as president part time while beginning my new job as the president of Brevard. Splitting my time between the two, flying back and forth was excruciatingly difficult. It was probably the most difficult time of my career. I had known my two predecessors at Andrew and trusted that the president who followed me would love the college as much as I did. Despite some hard feelings, we were honorees at a wonderful farewell reception at the college. Sarah Anne Staples and I remained good friends. She died in 2011 and plans for the dedication of the Sarah Anne Staples Biology Lab in Andrew College's Rhodes Science Center were announced the following year. That made me proud.

9

North Carolina Bound

In August 1985, my family moved to Brevard, North Carolina. While leaving Andrew College had been the right decision, I was nonetheless apprehensive. Had I done the right thing, not just for me, but for Fann and our three little boys whom I loved more than anything else in the world? I had been in my own little world and my family had made sacrifices for me.

In those days it was an 8-hour drive from the pancake-like terrain of Georgia to the blue-misted mountains of North Carolina, which gave Fann and me plenty of time to reflect on the major shift in our lives. I tried not to look back as we headed into the unknown. Our deep red Plymouth minivan, with fake strips of wood on the side, bucket seats in the front, and two bench seats in the back, was the perfect vehicle for a young family with three rowdy boys and Honey, our sweet Golden Retriever puppy. The minivan and a car-top carrier were stuffed with our belongings.

We were worn out near the end of our long journey, traversing steep roads that seemed narrow and treacherous to us flatlanders, so unused to rugged summits and deep gorges. One wrong move and we could plunge down a steep ravine. David, our youngest son, was so gripped with fear that he squeezed between the two bucket seats, whimpering, "We can't live in a place where we can't drive on the roads!" He had captured the anxiety we all felt.

We pulled into the Brevard College campus in the early evening. It was mid-August and the fall semester had not yet begun. We had brought sleeping bags, planning to spend the night in the president's house awaiting the moving van's arrival the next day. The one campus security guard was asleep in a broken-down Pontiac that was at least 15 years old. We exchanged pleasantries and I asked if he knew where we could find the key to the house.

He did not. We were exhausted. And locked out.

I was emotionally drained. I did not dare look at the boys and certainly kept from glancing at Fann. The anger I felt was red hot but I told myself to make an adventure out of this. We drove back to a pizza place we had passed on the way into town. After filling up on pizza we were refreshed and ready to head back to the campus. We sure didn't want to spend the night in the minivan. There was only one thing left for me to do: find an unlatched window on the first floor of the two-story president's house and climb in. I pushed through dense, waist-high, leathery boxwoods, pulled myself onto a window ledge, lifted the sash, and tumbled ungracefully onto a bedroom floor.

I was so glad that I did not face those hours being locked out without my family. When the moving van arrived the next day it began to feel more comfortable. Though it might seem humorous now, at the time there was nothing funny about the situation. The whole time I had been hoisting myself through that window, I was silently howling, "Be respectful of me and my family!" My feelings were hurt.

The first few hours, days, and weeks in a new relationship are vitally important, I later would advise colleagues. It sets the tone of one's presidency and it can take months of energy to overcome a bad beginning. Climbing through the window of my new home like a masked burglar in a cartoon was not the way to start a career move. No one at the college had volunteered to meet us—nor had I thought to ask. The stress of leaving Andrew and moving to Brevard had been intense. It never occurred to me to check to see if there would be someone to welcome us. It seemed all graciousness had slipped through the cracks. Where was Southern hospitality?

My mother could teach them a few things about putting out the welcome mat. For at least 40 years she chaired the hospitality committee at our church in Tifton. Every time a ministerial change came—and that is frequent in Methodist circles—she greeted the new family with a smile, fresh flowers, and a hot meal. Oh, how I missed my mother that evening.

Stories like this are not the end of the world, but it sure felt like it at the time. It taught me a valuable lesson. From that day forward we would see to it that new people felt welcomed and appreciated on the campus. How? We did that by forming a committee to greet families with food and a smile.

10

Grace and Gratitude

Our dog Gracie is smart and even-tempered. Fann named her Gracie because dogs are the archetype for unconditional love. Every day she reminds us of God's grace. One recent hot summer afternoon I didn't realize Gracie was standing right behind me. Without meaning to I stepped on her and hurt her foot, but without a second's hesitation, she came over and started licking me. That is Gracie. That is unconditional love and acceptance.

I have had a wonderfully enlightening theological education—Emory, Drew, and the University of Glasgow—yet for most of my adult life, the word "grace" has eluded me. At times I have felt that I was living in a state of grace. However, much more often I felt that the experience of grace was not to be found. Perhaps it has escaped me because it cannot be possessed. Grace is difficult for us Westerners to grasp. We are so sure that if we examine grace carefully under a microscope, we'll find the secret. Deep down, we believe if we are nice enough, thoughtful enough, generous enough, charming enough, and smart enough, grace will be ours. Grace essentially means we are accepted even though we are unacceptable. Theologian Paul Tillich in a book of sermons, *The Shaking of the Foundations*, writes:

> Grace strikes us when we are in great pain and restlessness. It strikes us when we walk through the dark valley of a meaningless and empty life. It strikes us when our disgust for our being, our indifference, our weakness, our hostility, and our lack of direction and composure have become intolerable to us. It strikes us when, year after year, the longed-for perfection of life does not appear, when the old compulsions reign within us as they have for decades when despair destroys all joy and courage. Sometimes at that moment a wave of light breaks into our darkness and it is as though a voice were saying: "You are accepted." You are accepted, by that which is greater than you, and the name of which you do not know. Do not ask for the name now; perhaps, you will find it later. Do not try to do anything now; perhaps later you will do much. Do not seek for anything; do not perform anything; do not intend anything. Simply accept the fact that you are accepted. (Tillich, 1948, pp. 161–162)

Those powerful words spoke to me personally and helped me as a college president. Sitting around waiting for someone to give me a compliment or a pat on the back and an "attaboy" probably wasn't going to happen. I had to have thick skin and realize I was accepted, and that nothing and no one was perfect. I tried to learn to be sure of myself and my efforts and not feel like I was being graded by how frequently or infrequently someone praised me. It helped to understand the value of relationships and I constantly reminded myself how paramount those are if our lives are to have value.

Our many summer vacations attending the Chautauqua Institution helped drive that point home. Chautauqua, a not-for-profit center in western New York that dates to 1874, offers a series of 9-week summer enrichment programs where current religious, social, and political issues are explored in the arts, religion, education, and recreation. Some 7,500 people are in residence on any day and more than 100,000 people attend public events throughout the summer. Among topics in 2022: "The Wild: Reconnecting with Our Natural World" and "The Vote and Democracy." Entertainment and speakers include Joshua Bell, Larissa Martinez, Fareed Zakaria, and George Packer.

I have had many life-shaping moments at Chautauqua. One was at a lecture by Irwin Kula, a nationally known Jewish rabbi and author who describes himself on Twitter as a "rogue thinker, disruptive spirit innovator." In his book *Yearnings: Embracing the Sacred Messiness of Life* (Kula, 2006), he tells a powerful story about ambition and lack of attention gone awry as a young rabbi in St. Louis. He was on a high, but Kula also talked of having what he called a "balance problem." There was always one more thing to do before he left the office, one more call, one more letter to write, one more sentence to add to a sermon. Even when the wonder of his position wore off, he didn't change and was chronically late. It had become a habit and he really didn't think much about it. He said he was always gracious and apologetic when he finally arrived at his destination. People knew he didn't mean anything by it and tolerated his bad habit, or so he thought.

Kula said it took a transfer to a new synagogue and a dinner in his honor at his current place of worship for him to learn a tough lesson about relationships, gratitude, and grace.

"My realization came just in time for me to begin a new chapter in my life," he recalled, "but it was incredibly painful." Kula had shown up nearly an hour and a half late to his farewell party. His friends and his wife were in the middle of their dinners. He made his usual round of apologies and again assumed his tardiness was no big deal. He walked around speaking to everyone but soon realized that no one was paying any attention to him. They continued their conversation, eating and drinking as if he was not even in the room.

Kula couldn't believe this was even happening. He kept trying to engage people and finally gave up, sat down, turned to his wife, and asked her what was going on. She told him how hurt everyone was by his continual tardiness, and one-by-one his closest friends laid into him about how insulting it had been to them for years. He was egotistical and self-important, they told him, and assumed that all should be forgiven. Weren't his wife and friends more important than any speech or any letter or writing any sermon could be? They were angry. The rabbi said he broke down in tears and apologized.

There had been little joy in his relationships but after the congregation's wake-up call, the rabbi understood that relationships come first and he did not have to be perfect. Grace had struck and he would be accepted for who he was, warts and all.

I like sharing two Christmas stories about the importance of the power of grace from the late Yale Divinity School Professor of Homiletics Halford E. Luccock. He taught many aspiring ministers and his words have been preached far and wide in countless churches.

In one tale, Luccock and a friend were sitting around the fire on a cold winter evening. His son Robert had telephoned to say the family was coming to visit the Luccock's New Haven, Connecticut, home over the holidays.

"Now, Robert, I want you to do some snooping around and find out what the girls want for Christmas without them knowing you're snooping," Luccock recounted. A couple of days later, his son reported the children "want the world"—a globe they could spin.

Luccock said he loved the idea. It was an educational gift and was something they'd always have to remember their grandad and grandmother. Luccock shopped and shopped until he found the perfect globe. He asked the store manager to wrap the gift and put a big red bow on the package.

Robert and his family arrived on Christmas Eve. After the girls had gone to bed, Luccock said he retrieved the globe from the attic and hid it behind the Christmas tree. The next morning, all the gifts had been unwrapped except one. "This is for you," he told his granddaughters. "Your grandmother and I love you very much."

The children tore into the package and lifted the globe out of the box. "Thank you, Granddaddy. Thank you, Grandmother," they said cheerfully and bounded out of the room to play with other gifts. He was puzzled by their responses.

That evening, as he tucked the sleepy children in bed, Luccock asked, "Would you tell your Granddaddy anything he asked you?"

"Sure," they replied.

"Grandmother and I thought we had given you the perfect gift but you didn't seem excited when you saw it. What did Granddaddy do wrong?"

The little girls fidgeted. After several seconds the older child told her grandfather, "You gave us a dark world and we wanted a lighted world." Their wish was for a globe with a light in it.

The next day Luccock dashed back to the store and exchanged it. When he brought home the new globe, he turned on the switch. The globe lit up and so did his granddaughters' faces. Recounting the story to his friend, he chuckled and said that the lesson he had learned was that a "lighted world costs more."

There are opportunities all around us to shine a light on people who live in darkness. If we're lucky, that glow—that grace—warms our hearts and lights the way when darkness engulfs us, too.

Luccock, who taught at Yale from 1928 to 1953, also liked to tell about a woman shopping for the holidays. Loaded with packages, she looked like an animated Christmas tree and spilled the gifts as Luccock happened to walk by. He picked up the boxes and bags.

"Oh, I hate Christmas, anyhow!" she said. "It turns everything upside down."

"That is just what it was made for," he told her. "Christmas is a story about a baby, and a baby's chief business is to turn things upside down. It is gross slander on babies that their chief passion is food, it's really rearrangement! Every orthodox baby rearranges everything he sees or can get his little hooks into, from the order of who's important in the family, to the dishes on the table. A baby in a family divides time into two eras, just as Christmas does. There is B.C., which means 'before child,' and A.D., which means 'after deluge.'"

Sometimes we can reach out to people with something as simple as a song or a sense of humor. When my friend Jock Lauterer and I were working together at Brevard College we came across a country song by Chris Stapleton called "Tennessee Whiskey." We both liked it. With apologies to Stapleton, I decided to sing it at the State of the College address.

> She's as smooth as Tennessee whiskey
> She's as sweet as strawberry wine
> She's as warm as a glass of brandy
> I stay stoned on her love all the time. (Dillon & Bartholomew, 2015)

It had nothing to do with anything other than getting their attention. Not taking myself too seriously continued to be important throughout my presidencies. During my tenure at Virginian Wesleyan, the headmaster of Norfolk Collegiate, a nearby independent day school for pre-kindergarten to 12th graders, asked me to speak at the dedication of their lower school building. The audience would be first-through-sixth graders.

The day came and I was dressed in my normal dark-colored business suit with a pair of black wingtip shoes. Just before the dedication ceremony I went into a school restroom and put my right shoe on my left foot and my left shoe on my right foot. Following introductions, I walked down from the stage to the auditorium floor where several hundred kids were sitting.

"Can you tell me anything funny about the way I'm dressed?"

"You've got your shoes on the wrong feet!" a fourth grader exclaimed. The place erupted with laughter.

"You can go through life without any education," I told them. "You don't have to learn how to read, how to do mathematics. Sure, you can make it, but that's all you're going to do, just make it. Education will broaden your horizons. I can wear these shoes on the wrong feet and it will hurt like the mischief and it will hurt every day but I'll be able to walk, maybe not as well, but I'll be able to get around. But it sure will feel better if I have the shoes on the correct feet."

Several years ago, I drove across North Carolina to give a speech at a little rural church in the middle of nowhere. Afterward, I chatted with several people from the audience. One little lady walked up to me, grabbed my hand, and cupped it in both of hers. With a warm twinkle in her eye, she said: "You are something. You are truly something. You just don't look like nothing." To this day I can't think about that without laughing.

Fann Dewar and Billy Greer met at the First Methodist Church in Valdosta, Georgia.

Former Georgia Supreme Court Justice Thomas O. Marshall, Jr., presents Greer with an award for his service to the state.

The Greers have always been family oriented and both parents tried to attend every sports or cultural event the boys took part in. From left, William III, Robert, Billy, Fann, and baby Benjamin.

The young Greer family, from left, David Benjamin, Fann, Billy, William III, and Robert Dewar.

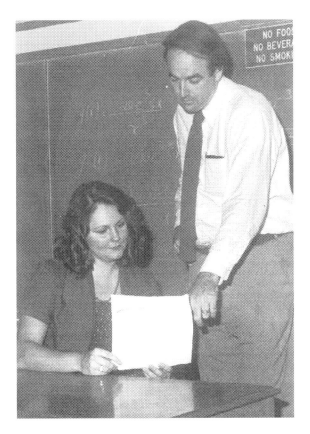

Greer and art faculty member Martha W. McKenzie work look over a project at Andrew College in Cuthbert, Georgia.

Former Florida Gov. Reubin O'Donovan Askew with Greer. Askew also was a state and federal politician who died in 2014 at the age of 85.

Andrew College in Cuthbert, Georgia, was founded in 1854 as Andrew Female College.

Billy Greer got good at cheering on graduates year after year during his tenure as president of Andrew College, Brevard College and Virginia Wesleyan University. All are associated with the United Methodist Church.

A retired Methodist minister, William T. Greer, Jr., was the president of three colleges and interim president of a fourth.

Bobbie M. Liggett, a faculty member in the Andrew College science department with the college mace and President Greer.

Andrew College president's home McDonald House, built in 1842.

First three VWC presidents at Investiture of William T. Greer, Jr. 1993. From left, Outgoing Virginia Wesleyan College President Lambuth Clarke, Greer, Former President Joseph Johnson.

Judge Jerry Bray, at left, Virginia Wesleyan University Board Chair, and Greer, 1993

From left, Governor Mills Godwin, Greer, and George Birdsong.

Groundbreaking for Virginia Wesleyan's Jane P. Batten Student and Convocation Center. From left, Henry Watts, Jane Batten, Frank Batten. In back, William T. Greer, Jr. excavator operator.

William T. Greer, Jr. shooting baskets with VWC women's basketball team.

Former Virginia Wesleyan President serves up a burger and hotdog at an Alumni Council Cook-out on Godwin Office balcony.

Virginia Wesleyan University, William T. Greer, Jr. at John Wesley bronze statue dedication ceremony.

Art student's portrait "Billy," 2015.

Groundbreaking for Greer Environmental Sciences Center, from left, Jane Batten, Greer, and Fann Dewar Greer.

Greer Environmental Sciences Center ribbon cutting at Virginia Wesleyan University. From left, David Kauffman, O.L. "Butch" Everett, William T. Greer, Jr., Gary Bonnewell, William D. Sessoms, Jr., Scott Miller, Mayard H. Schaus, and Linda Glover.

From left, Wiliam T. Greer, III, Robert D. Greer, William T. Greer, Jr., Fann Dewar Greer, David B. Greer

Billy & Fann.

11

Knowing When to Move On

I first learned about Virginia Wesleyan, another United Methodist Church-affiliated college, in the summer of 1982 while I was president of Brevard College. Lambuth Clarke, Virginian Wesleyan's president, and I were attending the Harvard Graduate School of Education's Institute for Educational Management, a multi-week session for higher education leaders. At the time, Virginia Wesleyan was two decades old, a mere academic infant compared to other Virginia schools like the College of William and Mary, founded in 1693, or Washington and Lee University, established in 1749.

"Billy, I've been with you in class," Clarke said one morning over breakfast. "Virginia Wesleyan is a young school but don't you overlook it; it's going places and so are you. I don't want you to forget about this college."

Clarke had been president of Virginia Wesleyan since the campus, situated on the Norfolk-Virginia Beach line, opened in 1966. Norfolk is home to the largest naval base in the world. Virginia Beach is a popular tourist destination known for its three-mile boardwalk and 38 miles of sandy beaches. By 2021, with a population of more than 450,000, Virginia Beach was the largest city in the state.

"I want you to keep it in your thoughts," Clarke continued. "I'm not going to always be there and I want you to think about it down the road. I'm going to retire at age 68 and I hope you'll still be interested in the school."

I was flattered by our conversation but we didn't stay in close touch. We only saw each other once or twice at meetings. Life went along, as life does.

When I had been at Brevard for seven years, Clarke announced his retirement but I had considered moving on to a more established institution. An opening for the presidency of Emory & Henry, a small United Methodist Church-affiliated college in rural Southwest Virginia, interested me. Meanwhile, Virginia Wesleyan was nibbling at my heels. They were all over me, something I had never experienced. Thomas B. Stockton, bishop of the Virginia Annual Conference of the United Methodist Church, personally called. In Methodist circles that's a big deal. He said he hoped I'd consider the Virginia Wesleyan job. I didn't pursue it. I was looking for a proven school, not one still wet behind the ears. Three or 4 months went by and one night Judge Jerry G. Bray Jr., a charter trustee and chair of the Virginia Wesleyan board, telephoned me at home. "You know we're interested in you," he said, "and we want to talk to you. I hope you'll express some interest. Bishop Stockton has said some nice things about you."

Emory & Henry was still my target and I again brushed off Virginia Wesleyan. Judge Bray reached out a second time. "Look, you need to come and at least visit with us." Fann and I talked about it that evening and the next morning Fann said she had dreamt something quite unusual. When you get a person who studies dreams talking to you about a particularly powerful dream you have to take notice—especially when she's your wife.

"In the dream, I had triplets," Fann stated.

Now that got my attention.

"We do need to pay attention to this dream," she said after we both stopped laughing. "I had these three baby girls and they grew into young adults in Virginia and that's important because it represents growth. Virginia Wesleyan is a young school that has terrific potential for growth."

Now she *really* had my attention. "You mean Emory & Henry?"

"No," she said, "you should rethink the call from Virginia Wesleyan and at least go visit and talk with them."

The college is built on 300 acres of farmland and is close to the Chesapeake Bay and the Atlantic Ocean. The more I thought about it, moving from a bucolic town to a bustling metropolis was preferable. Living near the ocean was another draw. At that point in my life, I was a pretty cocky devil. Moving to such a desirable area, while knowing absolutely no one, would be an exciting challenge. I was ready.

The entire two dozen search committee members, who represented a cross-section of students and trustees, met me in the college's Shafer Room. The interview had been in process for about 2 hours when Judge Bray asked if anyone else had questions.

"Billy, do you know anything about peanuts?" asked trustee George Birdsong of Birdsong Peanuts in nearby Suffolk. Unbeknownst to me, George was "the" Virginia peanut man. Unbeknownst to him, I had grown up in Tift County, Georgia, with summer jobs at the Coastal Plains Experiment Station. Assuming I probably knew a little more about peanuts than he thought, I rolled the dice and gave him a playful answer.

"Mr. Birdsong, I know peanuts don't grow on trees."

The search committee erupted in laughter.

Often, Northerners on their way to Florida would stop for gas in Tift County and many of the travelers were curious about how peanuts grew. As a joke the standard response was standard response was, "They grow on trees." And some of these folks probably believed it. Peanuts actually are legumes, not nuts, with their flowers above ground and the peanut beneath the soil. George Birdsong got a kick out of my impertinence and we still laugh about that conversation to this day.

By the end of the interview, I was thoroughly impressed with the people I'd met and their dedication to the college. Vice President of Student Affairs David Buckingham then showed me around campus. It was storming so badly that sheets of rain were slicing sideways, hardly a great day for a visit. We hadn't toured the campus long when a student came up to us and said Judge Bray wanted to see me. That's when I thought I must have really blown the interview.

Bray was waiting in the college's business office. A little guy with a high-pitched voice, Bray invited me to have a seat on a small sofa where only two people could comfortably sit and he plunked down beside me.

"Well, Billy, this has been an interesting day," Bray commented. "I want to thank you for coming."

Here it comes, I thought. I was being sent home.

"Oh, by the way," he teased. "We have found our president." He paused for effect. "It's you." This was a poignant moment. Judge Bray had been the board chair for many years. He felt responsible for the college's future. As he offered me the job tears were streaming down his face.

My mind was racing. "Judge Bray, I'm honored," I said, bewildered by the offer made so earnestly and so quickly. "My board at Brevard—they don't even know I'm here—and I need to go home and think about this and talk with my board chair."

"How soon can you get back to me?" he asked. I told him if he'd give me 48 hours he'd have my decision.

Fann and I went to the Norfolk airport to return to Asheville, the closest airport to Brevard. We didn't know a soul but while we were waiting for our flight someone called out my name. It was Virginia Wesleyan Vice President of Financial Affairs William T. "Bill" Joseph. He was returning the briefcase I had left at the college. "Bill," I said, "if I come here to be the president you'll probably be cleaning up after me all the time."

The offer of the presidency was tempting but I was still torn between going to a more established institution like Emory & Henry, which had been chartered in 1836, and a relatively new school like Virginia Wesleyan. Emory & Henry had been trying to reach me while I was being interviewed at Virginia Wesleyan, making the decision even more difficult. Bishop Stockton knew what was going on and I'm confident he whispered in Judge Bray's ear, "If Greer is who you want, you'd better seal the deal now because Emory & Henry is interested in him, too."

The judge and the bishop were good friends. When Bray spoke, I needed to listen. A lifelong member of Chesapeake Avenue United Methodist Church in Norfolk, Bray was prominent in United Methodist Church circles. He was an elected lay leader who served on most church committees, and a Sunday School teacher for more than 40 years. Bray also was the Virginia Annual Conference lay leader for eight years. From 1964 to 1992 he served as a delegate to the General Conference and also played an influential role at the general and jurisdictional levels of the United Methodist Church. He sat on the platform at the annual conference with the bishop and basically wrote the laws of the church.

The flight back home gave Fann and me time to talk about the pros and cons of leaving rural North Carolina for a corner of Virginia called South Hampton Roads. She had no desire to pick up and move from one sylvan area to another and I realized I didn't either. That was that. We ruled out Emory & Henry. Furthermore, I had appreciated the trustees' integrity, devotion to the college, and their appreciation for Lambuth Clarke's 26-year presidency.

I accepted the Virginia Wesleyan presidency on March 29, 1992. The school was young enough that I wouldn't be hearing "We've always done it that way" and there would be no fighting deep tradition. I'd also be in a metropolitan area. Within 24 hours I told the Brevard board chair I was leaving. Emory & Henry soon heard about my decision and the talk of going there faded into the woodwork; the guy who got the job became a good friend.

Our family moved to Norfolk, Virginia, the first week of August 1992, ready for a new academic year and a new chapter of our lives.

12

Knowing What is Expected

At the end of my first full day at Virginia Wesleyan, I joked with my assistant that it was time to leave work to "get in a traffic jam." Mary Knauer knew we had left rural North Carolina, which barely had a traffic light, but she had yet to catch onto my wry sense of humor. My cheerfulness, however, was short-lived.

Before starting the job, my office calendar had been filled for me, instead of by me, and it was out-of-hand in a well-intentioned effort to introduce the new guy to the community. Vice President of Advancement and College Relations Jim Bergdoll, a wonderful human being, jam-packed my date book before I even arrived on campus. I was naïve to give my calendar to Jim who had me slammed for 6 months with talks at Rotary clubs, churches—you name it. Of course, he did it to get me out there meeting folks. What I needed was to get to know students, faculty, and staff, but my packed schedule barely allowed me time to connect with anyone on campus.

A college president and his or her staff are responsible for leading an institution of higher education with input from the executive board.

However, I soon discovered it was the other way around at Virginia Wesleyan. That threw me for a loop. I hadn't realized when accepting the job that Board of Trustees Chair Judge Bray and the executive committee ran the school. Virginia Wesleyan was in its adolescence and Bray and its trustees felt responsible for it. It was their baby. Outgoing President Lambuth Clarke agreed the Board of Trustees had too much control, but he was very diplomatic and never came right out and said it.

The executive committee of about a dozen people gathered monthly and the full board—more than two dozen members—met twice a year. That was too many people and too many meetings. While trying to respect the college's culture and not demand changes right away, I put up with the existing meeting schedule for about a year. By then I had enough.

One day I said to Judge Bray, "When you have to put on the agenda of the executive committee where we're going to plant the next azalea, you've got the wrong guy."

He looked like a deer in headlights. "Tell me what you want to do and we'll do it," he said.

"Let me and my staff take the lead and cut down on the number of executive committee meetings," I said.

Judge Bray was someone who would listen, and he realized it was time for the school to grow up. He knew he didn't need to continue to run things but no one had suggested an alternative. We increased the number of full board meetings to three a year and cut executive meetings to one before each of the board meetings in the fall, winter, and spring.

The new structure worked beautifully and the addition of the third board meeting helped the judge know we still needed his involvement because he provided much-needed stability to all of us. Judge Bray would remain Virginia Wesleyan's board chair until 1995, for a total of 31 years.

Fann then, as now, was my voice of reason. As we planned our move from North Carolina to Virginia, we had to find a house and buy it. She casually asked, "What's your salary?"

I didn't know. Judge Bray and I never discussed compensation. I liked the place. It had tremendous potential with decent, civil people of integrity. In appreciation of his tenure the board had given Lambuth Clarke and his wife, Alice, the privilege of remaining in the college president's home. I liked that and assumed if they were fair with him they would be fair with me. That turned out to be true, but it was a mistake to have made such an assumption. This should serve as a warning to all persons accepting a position of leadership. Get the mechanics, fundamentals, and basics of salary, housing, and contract ironed out before accepting a position.

"Well, find out what your salary is," Fann said, exasperated.

It sounds like I was a complete idiot, but I was going with my gut. There was no formal contract for many years. There was never a contract at Andrew or Brevard, either. I figured if I didn't do my job, I didn't deserve to have the job. It's not the way to do business and I don't recommend it. I think it was a carryover from my time in the parish ministry. After I had been president of Virginia Wesleyan for some time, D. Henry Watts, retired vice chairman of Norfolk Southern Corporation and a long-time Board of Trustees member and chairman, asked me to stop by his office.

"We don't want you to go anywhere," he said.

"I don't want to go anywhere," I said.

"So what can we do to lock you up?"

"I like the idea of being locked up but you don't need to do anything; I'm fine." He drew up a formal contract that was mutually acceptable.

Moving to Virginia had been good for our family. For years Fann had been interested in the relationship between theology and psychology and knew she wanted to learn more. She decided to pursue a Master of Divinity degree from Union Theological Seminary of Virginia, in Richmond, and then went on to earn a PhD in clinical psychology from The Union Institute and University. She worked as a psychotherapist/pastoral counselor with Tidewater Pastoral Counseling Services in Norfolk for years before opening her own private psychotherapy practice.

Her graduate programs were rigorous. Richmond is 90 miles from Norfolk. Our lives were turned upside-down. Those three years when Fann drove back and forth to Richmond were the hardest of our lives, but she never missed getting home to have dinner with the boys and me. She would be worn out after a full day of classes, so most of the time she'd bring home "take out" or I'd cook something as long as she had planned it. David was big into basketball at Norfolk Collegiate. I don't think Fann ever missed one of his games.

Since Virginia Wesleyan was such a young school many of the staff and faculty had worked most of their careers at the college and felt a strong personal connection. They were an exceptional group of core faculty and staff who came to Wesleyan straight out of graduate school and stayed. Historian Stephen Mansfield and philosopher Lawrence D. "Larry" Hultgren were there when I retired. Mansfield joined Wesleyan's history faculty in 1968 and over four decades directed and edited the report for self-study of accreditation for the Southern Association of Schools and Colleges. He served as vice president/dean of academic affairs from 1995 to 2006; authored *Virginia Wesleyan College's First Half Century*, published in 2010; and he is the university's archivist. Larry Hultgren came to Wesleyan in 1969 as its first full-time philosophy professor and was a bioethics researcher at Norfolk's Eastern Virginia Medical School and Children's Hospital of the Kings Daughters. He founded and directed Portfolio, a program that connected the liberal arts with the world beyond the liberal arts. It included internships, extracurricular activities, community service, study abroad, and much more in order that the students could build a portfolio that could be presented to a prospective employer in hopes of helping them secure a job after graduation. He has also received multiple awards, and served as Wesleyan's representative to the National Collegiate Athletic Association for four decades.

As I met with different faculty and staff members in those first days of my presidency it seemed like an awful lot of us were named Bill. William "Bill" Gibson, a political science professor, soon became a colleague I could count on. Bill Joseph was vice president of financial affairs and a valuable member of our team. William M. "Bill" Wilson was our academic dean. William R. Shealy, a religious studies professor, was a Drew University graduate, who fortunately told his peers that the new guy had gone to his alma mater and that the college was getting a good president. He was so highly regarded by the faculty that putting in a good word helped get me off to a better start. The support of these staff and faculty members reassured me of being the right person for the job. Once while walking across campus with Dean Bill Wilson, he surprised me by saying, "God sent you to us." Wilson was not a gushy religious person but was deeply committed to his faith.

Another Bill—William Milton Jones—was a political science professor who became an informal dean and one of my closest friends. I physically towered over Bill, who was short, wore horn-rimmed glasses and bow ties, and drove a big antique Lincoln Continental. I first got to know him through committees and I saw him in action in faculty meetings. If tempers flared or it looked like we were at an impasse on any given subject, Bill would stand up and in his quiet way lead us out of whatever situation we had found ourselves in. I trusted his counsel—he would not let me make a mistake.

A film buff, Jones moderated a film-discussion series at Norfolk's Naro Expanded Cinema on Sunday mornings. He called it his "movie church."

Bill Jones understood my grandmother when I shared her advice, "Stir what you've got." He did just that every day of his life, in every endeavor he undertook. Students gravitated toward him and knew he would be their advocate. Other faculty were highly regarded, too, but Bill Jones was at the top of the list and I relied on his counsel.

A series of deaths among men I was closest to during my early years at Virginia Wesleyan affected me and the college community deeply. Dean Bill Wilson was killed in a traffic accident on Christmas Day 1994. The Wilson family had been on their way home from a worship service at Virginia Beach United Methodist Church. My family and I had just sat down for a festive Christmas dinner when Jim Bergdoll called with the devastating news. Edward "Del" Carlson was a political philosophy professor who had a strong interest in student development and inspired and directed the Freshman Seminar. After his death in December 2001 at the age of 54, the program was known as the First Year Seminar.

Lambuth Clarke, my predecessor, died in 2006, at the age of 82. I called him "Mr. Virginia Wesleyan" and had frequently phoned him to talk through difficult situations and to seek his wisdom. "How would you read this and that?" I'd ask. He'd say, "Don't let that person bother you, they've always been like that." Or, "If I were in your shoes I'd listen to her or him." Clarke was president the day Virginia Wesleyan held its first classes and for the next 26 years. His name graces the college's academic building, which gave Wesleyan the distinction of "one of the best-wired (Internet)campuses in the country" at the time it opened in 1998, but it is his legacy of integrity, civility, and focus on students that were his true mark.

I knew the school was in for some rough sledding when we learned Bill Jones had brain cancer. He died in May 2007 after a multiyear struggle with cancer and related illnesses. He was 62. As Bill Gibson said, Bill Jones was our true north. The college was evolving and Bill Jones was our shepherd. After he died, I wanted to look for an exit from the college and many times thought about doing it. I felt lost without him. He was so wise and had an insightful grasp of higher education law even though he did not have a law degree. I've never stopped missing Bill Jones. We lost our innocence when he died. It was a loss from which we never recovered. Rabbi Kula would have referred to these losses as "The Sacred Messiness of Life" which confronts us all at different times. It's how we deal with life's sacred messiness that makes the difference.

With Bill Jones, Lambuth Clarke, Del Carlson, and Bill Wilson gone I felt I had lost my four closest friends at work. They were my buddies. I like to think all five of us would classify ourselves as liberal Christians. Clarke said to me one time, "I hope I live long enough to see the word 'liberal' become a positive word again.'" By "liberal" he meant not being narrow-minded, but looking at the whole picture and accepting every one of any faith as though they are friends and brothers or sisters. Sometimes, even in the Christian church, we can get all hung up on who's right and who's wrong. We are all worshiping the same God. Theology is a man-made thing—a human construct. None of us has a corner on knowledge. We just need to get on with living together and working through issues. Those four men were cut out of that same bolt of cloth. Lambuth Clarke didn't get to see the word "liberal" become a positive word again.

I'm still waiting.

13

Humility as a Humble Servant

Growing a college is an enormous challenge. The needs are staggering: classroom spaces for the arts and music, practice rooms, theater spaces, playing fields and facilities for growing athletic programs, faculty offices, academic programs, library expansion, residence halls, dining facilities, activities areas, office space for administrators—not to mention endowment money for scholarships, and faculty and staff salaries. We stirred what we had while yearning for more to stir. Seventeen building projects followed while the endowment grew dramatically.

In the college's earliest days Lambuth and Alice Clarke spent untold hours working at forging relationships and community by engaging students in all sorts of activities from baking cookies to teaching students to play bridge. Yet no specific place dedicated to student activities existed. Years later after building Clarke Hall, the Trinder Center and Foster Field in 1998, and Godwin Hall in 1999, but there was still no student center. Frank Batten realized the need and delivered the transformative gift.

The $18.6 million, 137,000-square foot Jane P. Batten Student Center opened in 2002 and is named for Virginia Wesleyan Trustee Emerita Jane Batten. The center is the focal point of the campus with a convocation center seating 1,150, athletic offices, the chaplain's office, bookstore, student newspaper, and student counseling center. It has an eight-lane, 25-yard Olympic size swimming pool; three racquetball courts; a basketball court and three practice courts; three volleyball courts; an elevated jogging track; and a 36-foot climbing wall.

Jane Batten's husband, Frank Batten, was a pillar of the community who then owned the local newspaper, *The Virginian-Pilot*. Batten had built a media empire with Landmark Communications, Inc., which included The Weather Channel in Atlanta, the *Roanoke* (Virginia) *Times*, the Greensboro (North Carolina) *News & Record*, TV stations in Nashville and Las Vegas, *Landmark Community Newspapers* based in Shelbyville, Kentucky, and dozens of other media-related businesses. Saying he was a bold leader and big thinker is an understatement.

Jane Batten had invited Fann and me to a dinner party at their Virginia Beach home on a night when we were returning from Atlanta. I had been attending a winter meeting of The Commission on Colleges of the Southern Association of Colleges and Schools, the regional accrediting body for the 11 Southern states. A snowstorm canceled our midday return flight and we couldn't catch a plane until late on the day of the dinner. By the time we got to the Battens, everyone was having coffee and dessert and soon left. Fann and I didn't stay long and as we were walking out the door, Frank ushered me back to the dining room.

"I have an idea," he confided. "I'd like for you to come by the newspaper next week. This student center you've been talking about is a serious need. I'm going to give you $10.4 million for the project. Will that do?"

Screwing up my courage, I replied that a donation of that magnitude would "get us going." It jump-started the project and was the most important development toward building a student center. I often wonder if we hadn't made it to the tail-end of that dinner party if he would have sent the money anyway.

Having the student center named for Jane Batten, a leader in her own right, was monumental. Strong women in leadership make a difference. When I first arrived at Virginia Wesleyan it was a male-dominated place—call it narrow, chauvinist, misogynist—I'm not sure what kind of tag to put on it—but there were no women in positions of authority although there were some strong capable women on the faculty. The need was so glaringly obvious that I set out to correct it. There is much less wisdom without the feminine perspective.

When we lost our top adult studies person, we hired Katherine "Kate" M. Loring as director. Loring, who holds master of arts and PhD degrees in English from the University of Michigan, came to Virginia Wesleyan from Syracuse University, where she was senior program administrator for the Division of Continuing Education and Summer Sessions.

Kate endeared herself to me. We developed a relationship where she could say whatever she wanted and I listened. She was like a therapist. She'd say, "Billy, remember you have a lot of people sitting there in front of you who absolutely want to see the college succeed and only two or three are giving you a hard time. The rest are cheering you on."

Life has been cruel to Kate. Her daughter, Claire Cucchiari-Loring, 20, died in December 2006 after Claire's ex-boyfriend shot and killed her, before fatally turning the gun on himself. Cucchiari-Loring was a gifted vocalist studying at Old Dominion University in Norfolk. She had been a featured soloist at ODU's 2006 Jazz Choir concert. After her tragic death an annual concert, "Her Melody Lingers On," was held at the university in her memory with proceeds going to the Claire Cucchiari-Loring Memorial Scholarship.

Kate retired in 2013 as vice president for administration and special assistant to the president. In the many years we worked together she was not only my ally but mentored countless women at Virginia Wesleyan. Another strong woman was Board of Trustees member Rebecca Rogers, who remained on the governing body until she was in her late 80s. She was in charge of our board's elections and at one meeting announced the name of a new board chair without discussing any of the candidates. "Mrs. Rogers, where are the ballots?" I asked. "Oh, I destroyed them," she said, dismissing me as if I had just fallen off a turnip truck. The board thought little old Mrs. Rogers would never cause a problem. Little did they know what a renegade she was.

Many dedicated and outstanding women served on Wesleyan's Board of Trustees and faculty. I'll always appreciate history professor Marilyn Brady's vision and efforts for diversity by championing the addition of African American faculty and staff members, the Women's Resource Office, and offering Women's Studies courses, which grew into a Women's Studies major.

Sharon Payne directed the Women's Resource Office and spearheaded the effort to offer the Bachelor in Social Work degree, approved by the Southern Association of Schools and Colleges in 2012.

Kathy Merlock Jackson, now the senior woman faculty member and widely published author, is active in the American Culture Association having served as national president. She and Bill Jones co-edited *The Journal of American Culture* out of their Virginia Wesleyan offices for many years, beginning in 2002.

Linda Ferguson directed strategic planning and chaired the Social Sciences Division, becoming dean of The Birdsong School of Social Sciences. Joyce Howell, a PhD in art history, served as interim vice president for academic affairs from July 2006 to fall 2007. Deidra Gonzolas-Jackson, a bright young biologist, worked tirelessly to help us recruit diversity in the student body and the faculty.

Still, my one place of genuine disappointment was recruiting minorities for the administrative council and I only did a fair job of asking non-White members to serve on our board. The President's Leadership Council acted in an advisory capacity to the president and provided a forum for the exchange of information among the administrative staff and departments and with other constituencies. We'd court prospective job candidates and before we knew it they had accepted a more lucrative position elsewhere. The cynics would say, "You didn't want it to happen," which is not true. We would have been thrilled. We did have representation on the faculty, but not the administration. However, I was pleased that when I retired 24% of our student body were minorities compared to 6% when I arrived.

I am proud of my years as president of Virginia Wesleyan. We added major facilities such as the Jane P. Batten Student and Convocation Center, saw significant enrollment increases and the growth of the college's endowment, added a new four-credit curriculum focused on experiential learning, and established the Birdsong Community Service Program. Virginia Wesleyan was named a 2012 "Best College in the Southeast" by the *Princeton Review*. The Virginia Foundation of Humanities honored the college for significantly improving the quality of life in the Commonwealth. I was particularly pleased with the college's athletic accomplishments, including the 2006 men's basketball NCAA national championship. Athletics are vitally important, not only because coaching a strong team produces well-rounded student-athletes, but it also builds school spirit and adds significantly to campus life by providing multiple opportunities for the community to attend events and cheer on their team.

Those decades also were rewarding to me, personally. Along with the day-to-day challenges of running the college came involvement in the wider scope of higher education statewide and nationally. These associations not only made me a better and more focused administrator but gave me a wider view and a bigger pot to stir. The friendships and camaraderie among colleagues inspired and helped me to grow. Among other honors it was a privilege to be elected by my peers as a board member of the National Association of Independent Colleges and Universities (NAICU). I also was on the boards of the National Association of Schools and Colleges of the United Methodist Church (NASCUMC), a member of the Southern Association's Commission on Colleges, the Hampton Roads Partnership, Future of Hampton Roads, and the Lake Taylor Transitional Care Hospital in Norfolk where I served in various capacities. Former Virginia Governor Mark Warner appointed me to the state Board of Game and Inland Fisheries where I helped with the structure of the board. The Norfolk-Virginia Beach-Portsmouth Bar Association honored me with its Liberty Bell Award.

Upon reflection, a pivotal and transformative experience occurred earlier in my career. I was tapped by Leadership Georgia and honored to serve not only as a participant but also as program chair and later as president, and finally, chair of the board. At my retirement, the Virginia Foundation for Colleges named me a Lifetime Trustee.

My pocket calendar typically was chockablock with countless meetings. But I never begrudgingly sat through any of them acting like I was superior or knew more than anyone else. I look back on those boards and awards not with hubris, but with true humility as a humble servant who sought to do the best I could.

14

Collaboration and Relationships

At Andrew, Brevard, and Virginia Wesleyan, two key words constantly guided me: collaboration and relationships.

While it may sound elementary, relationships drive everything. In a workplace, there are good days and bad, joyful times and miserable ones, but without sound, affirmative relationships nothing moves forward and nothing is accomplished. Collaboration is just as important. In these days of limited resources, colleges need to set themselves apart from other institutions of higher learning and join forces with local and state businesses, schools, nonprofits, and community organizations. Relationships and collaboration can make a difference for any enterprise. I admire the advice of author and *New York Times* columnist Thomas Friedman when he advised not to think outside the box, but instead to think "without a box."

I found the "power of food" cemented relationships and created a culture of community and collegiality. Sharing a meal and conversation with others is one of the joys of life. After I held my first pig pickin' on the Andrew campus, I always made sure I had a gas grill within a few feet of my office. I don't know how many gas grills were worn out during my 37 years as a college president, but it was several. I entertained small groups of faculty, trustees, students, alums, and friends in the business community. On many occasions I have stood, apron at my waist and spatula in hand, flipping sizzling burgers or lean chops. An informal cookout was a great way to get to know people outside the confines of a stuffy office. There is something about inviting people to break bread with you that can take the edge off any discussion. Pig pickin' was a college-wide event, announced weeks in advance. The cooking started around 4:00 a.m. and we were pickin' barbecue 12 hours later. There typically was live music and always free T-shirts. It was a great time to build relationships and community. Even the herbivores loved it; we had veggie burgers for them.

One day I phoned a generous donor and asked him to lunch. There was what seemed to be a long pause. When he did finally speak he said, mournfully, "Billy, I can't come. You are going to grill me some salmon and then ask me for a donation and I'll end up giving it to you." He was right. He did come for lunch and I did ask for a gift to the college. He gladly contributed. There is no telling how many millions of dollars were raised from community benefactors as we chatted around a hot grill, whiffs of smoke teasing our tastebuds.

I am not suggesting that every college president or executive run out and buy a grill. That was my equivalent of doing business on the golf course or the tennis court. I tell everyone to find what works for them and use it to its best advantage. I sought ways to connect with people that made them and me feel a bit more relaxed. I can hear my grandmother saying, "Son, stir what you've got." That is to say, take the strengths you possess and the energy of your institution and its people, embrace that power, and build on it to form networks of support, both social and financial. Yogi Berra had it right: "You don't have to swing hard to hit a home run. If you got the timing, it'll go." I constantly looked for home runs.

Each college was different. At Andrew, we hired a staff person to conduct a summer day camp for kids ages 6–12. The Randolph County school system provided transportation for the camp and field trips. We charged a modest fee and offered scholarships. A local business underwrote the cost of T-shirts and the college provided a mid-morning snack and lunch. Camp counselors were area high school and college students. The program was a huge hit and filled a community need for children who were out of school and needed a place to go in the summer.

Brevard College partners with the nearby Brevard Music Center, an international summer institute and festival whose roots date to 1936 when a summer music camp was held for boys at Davidson College. The program was moved to Brevard in 1944. More than 500 students from around the country study for 10 weeks with 80 artists from orchestras, colleges, and conservatories, all under the direction of Artistic Director Keith Lockhart, principal conductor of the Boston Pops and chief guest conductor of the BBC Concert Orchestra in London. Tens of thousands of lovers of music—from classical to jazz, and bluegrass to opera—attend scores of performances by students and professional musicians. Past guest artists featured Yo-Yo Ma, Issac Stern, Itzhak Perlman, Joshua Bell, Conrad Tao, Jean-Yves Thibaudet, and Renee Fleming.

At Brevard, almost without knowing it, we also became a new business incubator for the arts. There were musicians, painters, photographers, and potters who wanted to start a business but didn't know where or how to begin. We would help them with the bread and butter side of their endeavor—for example, teaching a course on how to keep account ledgers. Oftentimes we'd provide actual physical space. Once ventures were up and running, they'd find a more permanent location and we'd move someone else in.

Brevard was small enough that if someone had an idea, we could sit around the table, talk about it and if it looked feasible we'd say, "Let's do it." Acting on a compelling idea required a measure of courage, but we were willing to give it a try. Some leaders are afraid and think if they take the plunge their board members might be up in arms. Believe me, those were risks worth taking.

Many of the most successful collaborations of my career took place during my tenure at Virginia Wesleyan. In 2009, we collaborated with the Virginia Aquarium & Marine Science Center to launch Ocean Explorer, a 45-foot research vessel outfitted for the coastal waters of the Chesapeake Bay and the mid-Atlantic. Designed for marine research, exploration, and hands-on education, the Ocean Explorer is a floating laboratory equipped with the latest technology and equipment. It features a flybridge observation deck, tuna tower, cabin with galley, V-berth, chart table, and an onboard computer system with Internet connectivity. Specialized equipment for marine research and a marine winch and crane are connected at the stern. Sophisticated equipment is used to measure the quality of the Chesapeake Bay water and its blue crab population.

Thanks to that partnership, Virginia Wesleyan added a new academic minor in marine science with a combination of biology and earth and environmental science courses. Oceanography, marine biology, ecology, environmental chemistry, and environmental geology classes use the research vessel for field trips, preparing students for graduate studies and a career in those fields. It affirmed the college's distinguished environmental studies program and spotlighted our high-energy faculty members. This eventually evolved into the signature program for the college—Environmental Sciences—facilitated by the gift of the Greer Environmental Sciences Center which was given at my retirement. This state-of-the-art facility attracts students from all over the country who come to study with equally outstanding faculty.

Glass blowing, surprisingly, was another wonderful opportunity for relationship building. One morning in 2012, I was having coffee with William "Bill" Hennessey, then-director and president of the Chrysler Museum of Art. The Chrysler is considered to be one of the major art museums in the Southeastern United States and is home to one of the leading collections of glass in the country, with more than 10,000 glass objects spanning 3,000 years.

As we sipped our coffee, Bill mentioned his interest in incorporating a glass-blowing studio as part of the museum.

"You have to find a way for Virginia Wesleyan to become involved," I insisted.

We quickly hatched a plan. The next thing I knew, a college van was dedicated to glass. Students enrolled in an art course called "Topics in Studio Art: Glass" and traveled to the museum's glass studio twice a week for an introduction to the practical mechanics of glassblowing, as well as the conceptual approaches to glass as an art form and the history of the medium.

Charlotte Potter, the studio's manager, also became an adjunct professor at the college. Half of her salary was paid by the college and half by the museum. At a special event and demonstration to show off the newly forged partnership, Potter deftly wielded a series of metal pipes tipped with glowing orange orbs of molten glass. With the help of several assistants, she demonstrated glassblowing's choreographed ballet. "There are things you can do on your own, but there's so much more you can do with a few friends," she reminded students. We really did make history by bringing together two dynamic institutions. It was cross-pollination that represented the essence of a liberal arts education. Not only was it a tremendous opportunity that benefited our students, but it also enriched the community as a whole.`

Another joint effort was with the local YMCA of South Hampton Roads to bring a climbing tower to the Virginia Wesleyan campus. The YMCA provided funding for the Alpine Tower in 2011 in exchange for use of land on campus. The tower is an imposing assemblage of massive wooden beams, ropes, swings, and platforms that stands 50 feet tall and weighs more than 18,000 pounds. The YMCA used the tower primarily in the summer for its camps and youth activities, while the college benefited from it for its

Department of Recreation and Leisure Studies classes, recreation activities, and team-building programs.

I also strongly believed that well-rounded students needed to make community service a priority. It was important to me that college be more than a knowledge "filling station." Sometimes when ideas are percolating, serendipitous things happen. One morning at Brevard, I received a call from long-time friend Sybil Dodson who was at the Open Door Community Center in Columbus, Georgia. It seemed she and her husband, John, wanted to move mountains. John had a growing pottery business. Sybil, a deaconess in the United Methodist Church and a fast-charging social worker by training, was completing a multi-year ministry as director of the center. She threw me a curve. "Billy, I want to come work at Brevard College in the housekeeping department. I believe I can do some good in the residence halls while cleaning the bathrooms, emptying trash cans, and mopping floors. I think the students will talk to me more if I'm working in that capacity rather than being an administrator."

I told Sybil she could not have called at a better time. "We are thinking about establishing a community service requirement here at the college. You are the perfect person to be the director." She agreed and the couple moved into one of the largest residence halls. Their son, Brad, joined them as a student-athlete and became a star runner for the cross-country team. He even won the national championship. At Brevard, community service became a rallying point for the students and was made a graduation requirement.

We couldn't have had a community service program without faculty and staff also taking part. Faculty are the single most important group of people on campus, aside from students, and they are with these young people regularly—when things are going well and when they're tough. We rely on our educators to provide support and to be role models for our students in service as well as academia.

Community service never became immersed in the academic program enough for it to become a graduation requirement. But it caught the imagination of a vast number of students. It caught on so well that we turned to philanthropist George Birdsong and the Birdsong family who gave seed money for the program and for the director, Diane Hotaling. A good example is Virginia Wesleyan Philosophy Professor Lawrence D. Hultgren, director of PORTfolio, a program open to all students and one that replaces a minor over four years. It is an effort to bring students outside the classroom and into the real world. Community service is a key component of the curriculum. Hultgren linked what students were doing academically with what they were doing outside the classroom. Some of the students helped with Hurricane Katrina relief in Pascagoula, Mississippi; staffed a homeless shelter; or tutored at a Title I elementary school. Students learn by doing in PORTfolio. They take field trips, shadow a professor in a three-week winter session course, and complete an internship. And it's no accident Larry Hultgren's classes were full. Throughout his career, he has been continuously interested in students both in and out of the classroom.

We even "stirred the pot" when it came to religion. Not unlike today, in the 1990s there was an awful lot of rancor and violence based on religion. I had heard on a national newscast that a car was pulled over by police because the officer thought its occupants were wearing masks and were up to no good. The driver was wearing a keffiyeh, the traditional headdress typically worn by Arab or Kurdish men. I didn't know the details, but the driver was shot by the police officer. After hearing about that horrific incident I met with my friend Robert C. "Bob" Nusbaum.

"It's time for people to stop killing each other in the name of religion," I said. Nusbaum, a Norfolk attorney and Hampton Roads civic leader, felt strongly about that, too.

Our meeting that day led to the September 1996 creation of the Center for the Study of Religious Freedom at Virginia Wesleyan College, with Nusbaum as its Founding Fellow. Nusbaum and his brother, V. H. Nusbaum, later established the center's Justine L. Nusbaum Endowed Lectureship in honor of their mother, widely known for her lifelong volunteer service and dedication to humanitarian causes.

In a letter to me, Bob Nusbaum wrote: "I venture to guess that more persons have been slaughtered in the name of religion than from any other cause... in this continuing saga of man's inhumanity to man, the one bright light that goes beyond mere tolerance is Jefferson's Statute for Religious Freedom. It laid the foundation for the First Amendment, and has served as a beacon for all enlightened constitutions ever since."

The center offers a forum for people of deep faith and abiding conscience, be they Jewish, Christian, Muslim, Hindu, Buddhist, Indigenous Americans, traditional African religions, or anything else, to share common goals that transcend denominational boundaries. The center provides a setting to find a common ground of mutual concern, working to achieve civil solutions to difficult problems.

Catherine Cookson, its founding director, brought the campus and community together in engaging and meaningful partnerships, addressing community controversies and challenges head-on. Dr. Cookson was an attorney and a religious scholar who advanced religious freedom through her monograph on the First Amendment, *Regulating Religion* and with her book, *Encyclopedia of Religious Freedom*. Both volumes are important resources for scholars and laypeople around the country.

From its beginning, the center was seen as a vehicle for fostering education and mutual understanding in our increasingly diverse world. Despite, or perhaps because of its goal of fostering engagement among diverse groups and faiths, it was like a lightning rod for some. We had one trustee who couldn't grasp why we were building bridges between Christian and Muslim communities. Individuals or groups sometimes cornered me saying, "I can't believe that you established something like this at a Methodist college campus." These people were suspicious of anyone who didn't look or worship like them. I'd tell them if Jesus were here he'd want to be on the center's board. Their jaws would drop and they'd realize they weren't talking to someone who would play the "ain't it awful" game. Creating the Center for the Study of Religious Freedom was the right thing to do and I wasn't about to back down.

It was important to build bridges not just between the campus and the community, but within the campus as well. I stuck to my guns. I could almost feel my father right there with me, just as I did every time I felt courageous and stood my ground. As a child, whenever I did something that we both knew was right, he'd affectionately say, "Billy Boy, way to go, Billy Boy, you hang in there." My Dad had courage. He read voraciously and was well aware of what was going on in the world. He was strong, knew right from wrong, and tried in his own way to make a difference; I've tried to do the same.

On September 11, 2001, 5 years after the center was founded, al-Qaeda terrorists attacked the World Trade Center complex in Manhattan and the Pentagon in Arlington County, Virginia. Nearly 3,000 people were killed and more than 6,000 injured after hijacked American Airlines Flight 11 and United Airlines flight 175 slammed into the North and South World Trade Center towers. Another plane was overtaken and plowed into the Pentagon. Hijackers grabbed control of a fourth plane, United Airlines Flight 93, and diverted it toward Washington, DC. Its passengers thwarted the fanatics and the aircraft crashed in a rural Pennsylvania field, killing everyone on board. The nation was stunned and horrified.

That night we held a tearful gathering of Christian, Jewish, and Muslim leaders, students, faculty, and community members at the Virginian Wesleyan dining hall, the biggest space we had. We desperately needed to comfort one another, bond, share our sadness, and renew our patriotism as we vainly attempted to understand why our country had been so viciously attacked. A student sitting next to me was in tears; her father had been killed in the Pentagon attack. I dearly hope we were able to console that grief-stricken young lady who lost one of the most important people in her life. That evening we were all brokenhearted. We sought each other out in those hours of uncertainty and we mourned together. It was a time to pray. And a time to weep.

15

Putting Out Fires

Becoming a college president was a dream come true, but I had to admit having students, faculty, staff, and community members look to me for all the answers was intimidating. After getting my head out of the clouds in that first presidency at Andrew, I learned some pitfalls went beyond the normal day-to-day expectations of enrollment, budgets, First Amendment rights, fraternities and sororities, and college security and safety. And those were just for starters.

Late one night the Andrew dean of students called me at home. "I need you to come to the hospital right away. We have a handful of drunk students and one of them has walked through a plate glass window. There's blood everywhere."

When I got to the emergency room, a half dozen of our foreign students were being treated. One teenager, still bleeding, unsteadily walked over to greet me. "It's so good to see you," he said, slurring his words. Then he took a swing at me. I ducked. He did it again. I ducked again. These kids were so drunk they could barely stand. Medical crews were furiously attending to the student who nearly cut off his arm crashing through the window.

These kids were from wealthy families and enrolled at Andrew to study English. Learning a new language wasn't foremost on their minds. Buying a Corvette and zooming around town was. They had ability, but at this stage of their lives they were not using clear judgment and weren't taking advantage of their educational opportunities. If sound judgment were leather, they wouldn't have had enough to saddle a June bug.

After the drunken night incident, we contacted the agency responsible for sending them to Andrew. "Listen, we weren't at all happy with the quality of the students you sent us." It was like placing an order for widgets. We'd get in touch with parents if there was severe misconduct and these kids surely didn't want mamma and daddy to know they had gotten in trouble. I can't recall if we sent any of those drunken students packing but we likely did. For other less serious misconduct, the dean took the keys away from more than one student's Corvette. So why did we put up with this nonsense? To be honest, they were cash-paying customers. And we wanted an international atmosphere on campus to broaden the lives of the American students.

That was just one of the many types of disciplinary actions I confronted.

In 2015, a fraternity's national office indefinitely suspended the Virginia Wesleyan College chapter for hazing violations. In an unrelated instance, a fraternity member broke into the college's maintenance building, found a key to the golf cart, and drove it slapdash into the nearby lake. That fraternity also was barred from campus.

Most fraternities and sororities do a lot of good, sensible things that benefit a college or university, but I found you have to get them on your side. If I started a new program, they were told their help was important. At Virginia Wesleyan, we launched a tutoring program for nearby elementary school children. Our fraternity and sorority students organized a schedule to feed children who probably would otherwise have gone hungry. After the college dining room shut down for the evening, students cooked meals for needy students, sealed them in containers, and took the food to the local Boys & Girls clubs where those kids came after school to eat dinner. In one year alone our students served the equivalent of 50,000 dinners.

Out-of-control and sometimes deadly parties make the news but there are a lot of good, smart, sharp young people who want to change this world. When I was that age I thought we were going to straighten out this country's mess. I had been in college during the turbulent '60s. Administrators ran institutions with an iron hand. Students typically had no voice. At Valdosta

State University the food was so bad we decided "these dogs don't hunt" and closed down the dining hall. Virtually the whole student body plopped down in front of the dining hall one day. I was leading the sit-in and protest. In hindsight, it was a stupid thing for us to do when so many people don't have anything to eat. The food did get better, though.

Another time a group of us paid a visit to the president's office at Valdosta State because students were being charged a fee for photos for identification cards and we were supposed to get the money back. Most of the time that didn't happen. Alas, our complaints didn't correct the problem.

As a college president, I worked hard to communicate with students to let them know what was going on and what might happen down the road. When we got into rough times, my door was open.

I believe in freedom of speech, but not hate speech. My motto: say anything you want, just make sure it's factual and within the bounds of civil discourse. Yes, we have to make our institutions places where free speech is part of the day. But there are limits. I refused to allow Ku Klux Klan members to speak at Virginia Wesleyan. Ours was a private college so I could—and did—veto hate groups like that on campus. White robes? Burning crosses? Not at our college.

Unfortunately, public, taxpayer-funded institutions of higher learning don't have that luxury and can rack up bills in the hundreds of thousands of dollars to pay for security when a controversial speaker is invited. Racism did not go away with the election of Barack Obama, our country's first Black president. It only burrowed underground and is now resurfacing with a vengeance and is all but being condoned by some of the nation's highest elected officials.

So where should the line be drawn between free speech and hate speech and who should be allowed to make that decision? I don't envy college presidents who have to determine whether to allow people onto their campus who spew hate. I could make the call to keep them out and the board and faculty backed me.

Sometimes hatred is more subtle. Some years ago, a young development office staff member and I paid a call on a Virginia Wesleyan graduate and successful Norfolk businessman. During our conversation he blasted me and the college asserting, "Virginia Wesleyan didn't have any niggers until you got there and it's going to wind up being just like Norfolk State University," a historically Black Virginia college established in 1935.

That was all I needed to hear. I abruptly stood up. "You know, there's no reason for us to have any further conversation," I said. We walked out. I hope one day that young development officer might have the same reaction if she's in a similar situation. I like to think that if this guy had offered me money that was not earmarked for something distasteful, I'd take it and give scholarships to Black students. But he might have said he was going to give us a half-million dollars to build an institute for Whites only. I'd tell him to keep his money.

During my first presidency at Andrew, I invited Julius S. Scott, Jr., as our commencement speaker. Over a long career, Julius was president of Paine College, Wiley College, and Albany State University—all historically Black institutions of higher education. You didn't have to be very-dark skinned to be despised by a lot of people in the deep south, and nationally. One of Andrew's major donors got angry and withheld funds. Scott delivered a powerful and inspiring speech to our graduates and I was thankful he gave it.

Yet none of those stories held a candle to the two most devastating situations I encountered in nearly four decades as a college president.

In 2006, a Virginia Wesleyan security guard was murdered and his assailant has never been found. As heinous as that murder was, it could have been even more catastrophic.

A group of about a dozen young women (sorority sisters) stayed on campus over a semester break. On that fateful night they were playing hide and seek in the dining center without realizing someone had slipped into the building. That person—we don't know if it was a man or a woman—found a cash box with a small amount of money at the same time Walter Zakrzewski, our unarmed security guard, walked in. The intruder ran with a butcher knife from the dining hall kitchen, chased the guard, and killed him, nearly cutting off his head. Zakrzewski died tragically but unknowingly may have saved the lives of these young women.

In 2012, a first-year Wesleyan student alleged she had been raped by a classmate during freshmen orientation. Both had been drinking. The male student was never criminally charged and the young woman did not file a complaint with the police. She did see the college counselor, who encouraged her to file a police report, but she never did.

The young woman later sued the college for $10 million, insisting the college was negligent in protecting her. It took 4 years of legal wrangling but a jury unanimously sided with Virginia Wesleyan. Three days after the alleged rape, the woman had been asked by a friend on Facebook why she was so upset. The alleged victim replied: "I was so upset because he was ugly." The attorney told a local TV station that the line of questioning about that response "was powerful for the jury."

We had followed all our rules to the letter and the court believed we did, too. There were no winners. Everyone lost. Our policies were solid and had been carried out to the nth degree. Still, we invited professionals to look at the campus from a 30,000-foot level to determine if there were additional ways to improve the safety of our students. We installed more lighting and call boxes and added more officers on bicycles, especially during the evening hours. These two young people were just kids. They made bad choices and they paid the piper. Unfortunately, we all suffered and the college was tarred with unwarranted publicity.

The heinous fatal attack on our officer and the unfounded rape allegation hit me harder than a ton of bricks. I still brood about both heartbreaking tragedies. Times have certainly changed as violence proliferates nationwide. In 1980, Andrew College had one security officer who carried a big flashlight. His shift started at about 5:00 p.m. and he stayed until about 10:00 p.m. We thought of the place as being secure. When I came to Brevard we had a lone security guard who nightly drove around campus in his old, beat-up Pontiac. Those colleges were small and rural. Even back then Virginia Wesleyan was in a metropolitan area and had several police officers, all on foot. Today there is an entire police force on its grounds.

College presidents, especially those new to the world of higher education, also are faced with challenges that are certainly less traumatic and hateful but important. How to handle declining enrollment is one example. If someone in leadership is working at a small-to-mid-sized liberal arts college in this country, chances are a decline in student enrollment can be significant. It's how challenges are dealt with that matters.

About 5 years before I retired, we had an unusual dip in the student population at Virginia Wesleyan. We expected a freshman class of about 400. That first year we probably had 300 students and for a small school, that's a big drop. The next year we were down about another 25 students. I hadn't mashed the panic button but I was looking for one to mash. There are companies around the country that provide help with enrollment and after doing my research and talking to colleagues, we hired a national group. These companies aren't cheap. It was a couple of hundred thousand dollars a year on a 2-year contract. Sometimes consultants like this produce and sometimes they do not. They did well for us.

We got the enrollment back up by changing our marketing and packaging new scholarships. They helped us develop a strategy to promote our college in Pennsylvania where we picked up a lot of new students. We had been marketing in New Jersey but pushed harder. The next year our enrollment soared and the following year it climbed again. Some colleges add athletic programs such as football and swim teams hoping for that silver sign-up bullet. We didn't have the kind of money to give a student a free ride but we cut the price for less financially able students—discounting it's called in the profession. Recruiting from community colleges also helped. For the first time in their lives, some students got a toehold at a 2-year college and landed on their feet. It changed their lives.

Staying financially sound was a major challenge. I was always obsessed with budgets and in all those years we never had any red ink. But in my early days at Virginia Wesleyan, we had some really tight budget problems. Once, my finance guy came to me and said, "We're going to be about $10,000 short." Two or three days after our conversation, the president of the Hampton Roads Automobile Dealers Association telephoned. He asked if the grounds at the college could be rented for a weekend car sale.

"What would you charge us?" he asked.

"Ten thousand dollars," I told him.

At the end of that event, they stroked us a check for that amount. It looked like a pretty good deal because it was a way out of a budget issue. It wasn't that simple. A nor'easter tore through the region that weekend, wreaking havoc on the campus. Four hundred to 500 new cars got stuck in grassy areas that turned into a sea of mud. Tractors spun their wheels in the muck to drag the once-shiny vehicles out with chains. To say it was a mess was an understatement. The faculty was up in arms and wanted to know who in the world authorized the event. I went to the head of the automobile association and told him the damage had to be repaired. I have no idea what it cost but they fixed it.

Sometimes it was better not to get my knickers in a knot. One biting cold winter night at Brevard, 50 or 60 students were helping me barbecue a pig. We were all trying to stay warm by the fire, our mouths watering with the thought of fresh barbecue. Suddenly, this buck-naked kid came out of the side door of one of the dormitories not more than 10 feet from us and bolted down the campus. "Streaking" was popular back then and somebody asked, "Who's that?" "That's just John" was the reply and none of us paid any attention to him. If you're going to work with young people it helps to have a sense of humor.

We had bigger fish to fry although some trustees and faculty no doubt thought something like that was a pretty serious offense. In this case, I had to fish or cut bait, so to speak, and to me a student running bare-butt past us wasn't the end of the world. Even when there is a conflict we don't always know how to go about working our way through it or when to sound the fire alarm. I don't know why that is, and of course, it's not just peculiar to higher education. Sure, we often can do a better job of putting out fires, but sometimes you have to just let them burn.

16

Stewardship

Why it Matters

It sure seems like Ivy League colleges and universities have more money than God. Harvard's endowment topped the list at nearly $53.2 *billion* at the end of the 2021 fiscal year. Some joke Harvard is a hedge fund with a university attached. Yale was at $42.3 billion for the same time period and Stanford had $37.8 billion of donated financial assets. They are the big guys with big names, big donors, and bulging wallets.

Endowments—at any size institution of higher learning—are financial foundations that help fund student aid, teaching, new buildings, research, the arts, public service, and athletics. A cache of money is invested to grow the principal and provide additional income for future investing and expenditures. Not more than 10% of the country's colleges and universities have unlimited resources. Many of the rest—especially small colleges—are challenged to stay alive.

In the early days at the colleges I led, we had to be good stewards of our resources just to keep the lights on. The pool of givers typically was small and many times we'd ask for help and get a cold shoulder or we'd be outright turned down, even by our own board members. Some trustees were local residents but not alums and frequently their loyalty was first to their own alma mater and other institutions. For others, the title of college board trustee was only a hobby that came with prestige and social status. Some people give money because they want to check a box and see their names in print to impress their friends and neighbors. Others truly are honored to serve and can understand the need to help young people. They genuinely want to support the arts, aid students with limited financial resources, fund research, establish professorships, or help expand a college's footprint.

Who are the supporters of a college, or for that matter, of any good cause? I like to say it's those men and women who had good mamas and daddies. Their parents taught them to give back. Even little children should be taught about stewardship. They don't know what that means so when I'm sitting beside one of our grandchildren in church, I'll take a dollar out of my billfold, fold it up very small and tell them I'm giving it to them to put in the church offering plate. If the church is building a Habitat for Humanity house, I might give the children money to donate toward that project. I trust they'll grow up to give back to their communities and their causes.

It's something I learned as a child. John Wilson, our Methodist minister in Tifton, Georgia, was raising funds for a new church. He told me each brick cost a nickel and if I put a nickel in the offering plate every Sunday, I'd be doing something very important. I saved nickels from my allowance and from everywhere I could find a coin. The lesson was to be a good steward and I've never forgotten it. It made me feel special. If I have a generous spirit it can be traced to my upbringing. My father gave money to people who needed it. At his funeral, two young people arrived in work clothes. None of us knew who they were but we looked at each other and said, "We guarantee our Dad did something to help those people."

What is stewardship? I can best describe it with a story. I was sitting at my office desk one day at Virginia Wesleyan with a donor who was offering the college a major gift. I thanked the donor profusely who then asked "What do we get for all this?" I wanted to say, "I'm giving you your money back." That wasn't stewardship. There's no joy in that. Stewardship is an attitude.

Development, on the other hand, is putting together a plan or a strategy for addressing needs. It is raising money for a worthy cause. Stewardship is caring about the world around you and the people in it. It's a very close kin to development but it's not the same thing.

Business leaders and college presidents must cultivate donors to be good stewards. You'd be amazed at the number of executives who make an appointment with a potential supporter, get a contribution and fly out the door looking for the next gift. They don't spend enough time on the front end—or the back end—with donors who can choose to spend their money any way they want. They decline to pay attention to their donor base or to keep good records.

Most people dread knocking on doors to ask for money. Developing relationships with benefactors and potential givers and cultivating those ties has always been my favorite endeavor. It's something I did well because I loved the schools I led and had the patience, optimism, and humility to cultivate those folks who provided the financial means to keep us viable. Somehow I was able to share my dream with them.

We're at our best when we don't see ourselves as extracting something from somebody. It's not just being nice to people because they have a zillion dollars and they'll do something good. It's understanding that each donation is a special gift to be appreciated, invested in, and used wisely.

Anyone who takes sole credit for a major gift is foolish because it's all about teamwork. As simple and corny as it sounds, financial growth is advanced not just by a college's development office, but by students, faculty, and colleagues who tell the story about the school. When honored with a gift of any kind, it was because of what we all had done to bring people closer to the institution. We wanted those contributors to fall in love with the college by helping them learn and understand the school's mission, vision, and needs. It is hard work. Talking to potential benefactors about their interests sometimes took decades. I patiently waited and matched their interests with a project at the college.

My first presidency was in one of the most economically depressed areas of southwest Georgia. Our children went to school 35 miles from home and major shopping and medical services were more than an hour's drive. When I arrived at Andrew in June 1980, the college could barely make ends meet. It was Cuthbert's largest employer but most of its trustees and contributors were not closely tied to the college and lived in bigger Georgia cities like Atlanta, Columbus, or Albany. My goal was to build relationships outside the rural community and it was not uncommon for us to entertain prospective patrons at picnics in Atlanta's Chastain Park Amphitheatre—150 miles away. We had four season tickets and we'd invite a couple to join us whose friendship we enjoyed and who may have wanted to get involved with the college. The invitations were well received because entertainers like Joan Baez, Johnnie Cash, Andy Williams, and the Atlanta Symphony Orchestra performed at the park. Even when we were trying to hire new faculty, we would meet them in Atlanta or another city and tell them how wonderful it would be to teach at Andrew College before asking them to meet us on the campus miles from a metropolitan area.

With careful investing by one Andrew board member the college's endowment grew to at least $5 million by the time I moved on. I had met M. G. "Woody" Woodward and his wife, Connie, when I was pastor of Forest Hills United Methodist Church in Macon, Georgia. Woody and Connie had the reputation of being extraordinarily generous and benevolent people. They had adopted seven children, most of them considered unadoptable. Woody was considered a financial genius. During his long career, he managed the Joseph Kennedy and the Sears family estates. When Fann and I met the Woodwards they were reaching retirement age. They had moved to Macon, where Woody managed Charter Medical Corporation, a growing chain of psychiatric hospitals. True to their reputation for generosity, they were generous supporters of the church and when I became president of Andrew, I asked Woody to join the college's Board of Trustees.

It's not an overstatement to say the Woodwards almost single-handedly transformed the college. My team and I always had an idea a minute about what we wanted to do to help the college but we had no money. "How much will it take?" Woody would ask and he'd make the lead gift to underwrite the project or contribute serious dollars to construct new facilities. I came to realize I'd better not ask him to consider funding everything because he would do it and I didn't want him to think I was trying to take advantage of him or our friendship.

Bill Turner, the Char-Broil creator, was a wealthy, humble philanthropist who also supported Andrew. Many of his gifts to Andrew were anonymous. So were those from the Woodwards. They taught me—I don't know how—not to feel intimidated by wealth. That turned out to be a treasure in itself.

I learned that cultivating relationships can be rewarded in unusual ways. While at Andrew, I attended the inauguration of a new president of Wesleyan, Fann's alma mater. The Macon college was held in high esteem in Georgia and as the president of small fry Andrew College, I was feeling a little out of place that day. During the reception, I mingled with guests and enjoyed talking with Boisfeuillet Jones, whom I knew through his daughter, Laura Jones Hardman. Jones had held numerous positions at Emory University, served Presidents Kennedy, Johnson, and Carter, and headed philanthropic foundations, including the Emily and Ernest Woodruff Foundation and the Robert W. Woodruff Foundation.

"Oh by the way," he said, almost as an after-thought. "I've got some extra money and I'm going to send you some next week." True to his word, I got a check made out to Andrew College for $50,000. It may not be much by today's standards but back then it was like a million dollars to that little school. Jones saw me as a fledgling college president and knew Andrew College well enough to understand it was struggling every day. We put the money in our general scholarship fund.

The most impressive building on the Andrew campus was the McDonald House, a historic Greek Revival mansion that served as the Andrew president's home. It was built in 1848, enlarged in the late 1880s, and given to Andrew College for the president's residence in 1976. When we lived there Fann took charge of renovating and redecorating the interior. I have no idea how large the home is—it is huge with very high ceilings—but a testament to its size is how many rolls of wall covering were needed in the downstairs entrance hall: 106. By contrast, when we moved to Brevard and lived in the home designated for the president, 27 rolls of the same wall covering were needed for a similar entryway.

The McDonald House was the drawing card Andrew College needed. People were curious about it and wanted to visit. Fann planned receptions, dinners, surprise birthday parties, musical soirees, Easter egg hunts—anything she thought people might be interested in attending in hopes of getting people to visit Andrew. Representatives of the Lettie Pate Whitehead Foundation, the Robert W. Woodruff Foundation, the Tull Foundation, the Bradley Foundation, and others were all invited to Andrew College dinners or events. The house became the social hub of the community but it was a bear to maintain and we always had someone making repairs. Even though it was a drawing card for visitors, the college needed the expense of its upkeep like a hole in the head.

During my tenure at Andrew, I was a participant in Leadership Georgia, one of the oldest training programs for young business, civic, and community leaders. The next thing I knew, I was on the executive committee and later president and chairman of the group. One of my good friends at Leadership Georgia was Sally Blackmun, one of three daughters of the late Supreme Court Associate Justice Harry Blackmun, most remembered as the 1973 author of *Roe v. Wade*, the decision that made abortion legal.

"Can we get your Daddy to speak at our fall convocation at Andrew?" I asked Sally. A Skidmore College and Emory University School of Law graduate, Sally asked her father, who agreed.

We spiffed up the place for an outdoor reception, including moving some ligustrum shrubs to the back for a hedge. They died. Undaunted, we went to the hardware store and spray-painted the moribund ligustrum dark green. They provided a background and no one noticed they were dead.

We had an associate justice of the U.S. Supreme Court coming to a no-name place in the middle of nowhere. We invited members of the Georgia Bar Association and it seemed like every attorney came to hear Blackmun's speech. At dinner, Fann comfortably seated 27 people in the banquet-sized dining room. Andrew College made headlines.

Weeks later, our middle son, Robert, was learning the names of the U.S. Supreme Court justices in his fifth-grade class. When the teacher got to Harry Blackmun's name, Robert raised his hand. "Yes, ma'am, I know him. He is a friend of my family. He spent the night at our house. I saw him in his underwear." His teacher didn't believe him and thought he was being a wise guy. We've had a lot of fun with that story through the years. Blackmun was a down-to-earth man who was not puffed up. To him, it was about attitude, not altitude. He drove a Volkswagen Beetle to his Supreme Court offices. When he died in 1999 at the age of 90, that VW bug was in the funeral procession.

Dean Rusk, the U.S. Secretary of State from 1961–1969 under Presidents John F. Kennedy and Lyndon B. Johnson, also was a speaker at Andrew College. Rusk had his own underwear story. He was born in rural Cherokee County, Georgia, and according to one newspaper account, as a small boy, he ran around in underwear made from flour sacks. Rusk returned to his native Georgia in 1970 and taught international law at the University of Georgia School of Law in Athens.

Andrew had an honor society that was well-thought-of nationally. I said to my colleagues, "Why don't we try to get Dean Rusk to speak?" I drove more than three hours in a torrential storm to Athens, Georgia, went to his office, and introduced myself.

"We'd like you to come to Andrew College in Cuthbert, Georgia to speak," I said. He turned to his secretary. "Bring me a map, I want to find out where Cuthbert, Georgia is." He looked at the chart and said sure, he'd do it. A lot of people were surprised that the man who had been front and center during both the Cuban Missile Crisis and the Vietnam war would come to itty bitty Andrew College. Rusk retired from teaching in 1984, a year before I moved on from Andrew. He died a decade later.

Georgia native Griffin Bell, President Jimmy Carter's attorney general, also visited Andrew at our request. Bell had earlier been appointed by President John F. Kennedy to the U.S. Court of Appeals Fifth Circuit. The *New York Times* wrote that Bell, who died in 2009 at the age of 90, had been "a strong defender" of the First Amendment, opposed segregation and discrimination and racial quotas.

How'd I get people like Harry Blackmun, Dean Rusk, and Griffin Bell to come to little Andrew College? I simply asked them.

For another visitor to the Andrew president's house, it was personal. Gertrude Castellow Ford grew up in the McDonald house. She was the daughter of the late Bryant Castellow, a U.S. congressman, educator, and attorney, and Ethel McDonald Castellow. Gertrude, born in 1913, was 14 when her mother died. She came from a wealthy family who earned their fortune in the timber business harvesting local pine trees. A $25 donation from her family more than 165 years ago helped launch what was then the Andrew Female College Building Fund. The college's first students enrolled in 1852. Gertrude moved to Mississippi when she married Aaron L. Ford, who like her father, was a congressman. Gertrude had a deep passion for the arts, played several musical instruments, loved poetry and literature, and spoke four languages fluently. She was raised in the tradition of philanthropy, but something happened—no one knew what—and she was estranged from Andrew College. For decades the Andrew College leadership had reached out to her in an attempt to mend the broken relationship.

In 1983, Gertrude Ford returned to Cuthbert to bury her recently deceased husband. She wanted to visit her childhood home and was staying with a lifelong friend who called Fann asking if Gertrude could come for a short visit of her ancestral home. Fann urged her to visit but asked for 30 minutes to straighten the house and then started throwing things into closets and under beds. The doorbell rang, just as our friend and six little boys dashed out the back door. Mrs. Ford had a wonderful time reminiscing about her childhood while visiting her family home. The "short" visit kept extending. As time for the funeral service approached out of town guests began to arrive.

The Ford family and long-time acquaintances had traveled great distances to be with her at the cemetery and apparently recognized her car parked in the driveway of the home where she had lived as a girl. They stopped and all paraded into the house. Soon the crowd had grown fairly large with people sharing memories of Aaron Ford and reminiscing about old times in the house.

When it was time to go to the cemetery the assembled group left. Fann felt she had hosted a wake for someone she had never met. But that kindness changed Gertrude Castellow Ford's attitude and was the beginning of a much more congenial relationship between her and Andrew College. In 1991, she established the Gertrude C. Ford Foundation in Jackson, Mississippi. At her death in 1996, Andrew College received a bequest of $8 million, the largest gift in its history. In 1998, the foundation awarded The

University of Mississippi $20 million to design and build the Gertrude C. Ford Center for the Performing Arts and at least another $35 million to Ole Miss. Gertrude Castellow Ford is buried in Cuthbert beside her husband.

You never know when an act of kindness might be rewarded. A devoted member of our Brevard College housekeeping team stopped by my office and told me she had just learned that cancer was ravaging her body. She tearfully asked if she might continue to work in some capacity at the college. I assured her she could.

Shortly after her death, a woman from the community asked to see me. She struck me as affluent and well-dressed and told me our housekeeper had a second job working for her and often spoke of her gratitude that the college continued to support her with a job and a paycheck. "Because this is a place that cares so deeply about its people, I intend to leave everything I have to Brevard College," she said.

Think about it—one of the largest gifts ever received by that college did not come about because of the brilliant leadership of the president or the development office. It was because of a relationship. No one can whistle a symphony. It takes an orchestra.

I learned that presidents of colleges, universities, corporations, businesses, or nonprofits have to tread lightly around wealthy and powerful people and their money, which can be especially intoxicating. In working with boards in the development and fund-raising efforts, in representing an institution in all kinds of settings, there are plenty of opportunities to hang out with the rich and famous. Nothing will damage a presidency more than if its benefactors see them wooing people with big piggy banks while ignoring those who have meager bank accounts. For me, that wasn't difficult because I was a small-town country boy who had been blessed with opportunities to climb my own educational and professional ladders.

Early one morning when I was a neophyte college president at Andrew, I drove several hours to Atlanta for an appointment with J. Pollard Turman, chairman of the Tull Charitable Foundation whose grants are limited to Georgia. I went to his third-floor office and told him Andrew's best days were behind it and that we were now trying to bring the school back to life but needed financial help. The Tull Charitable Foundation had never given a gift to the school. After a brief conversation, I asked for $100,000, thanked him, and left. To my horror, I saw my car with its back wheels hoisted on a tow truck in the building's parking garage. I ran over to the driver.

"Sir, what's the problem?" I asked. He told me I had parked in a reserved space.

"There's no sign saying I couldn't park there," I stammered.

"You can see where there *had* been a sign," he said indignantly. "You can pick your car up at the pound."

I pleaded. "I've been upstairs visiting Mr. Turman. Give me five minutes." I ran up the steps to the third floor. Turman was in his outer office talking with his secretary.

"Mr. Turman," I said in a panic, "my car is downstairs about to be towed and I have a 4-hour drive back to Cuthbert. If you want to give me a down payment for the gift I requested, please give me a twenty-dollar bill." Instead, Turman and I rode down the elevator together. Sure enough, there were no signs indicating a reserved parking space. The guy driving the tow truck looked sheepishly at Turman, lowered my car and I was on my way.

And yes, the college got the $100,000 gift. When I saw my car partially on that wrecker there was nothing I could do but be myself. I couldn't walk back into Mr. Turman's office and make up some story. Turman saw me as an all-right kind of guy who was not trying to tap-dance on him. That's likely not the only reason we got the gift but I don't think it hurt.

Funding for any proposed project also had to "ring true." A donor had to hear my presentation and believe I wasn't trying to simply extract dollars from them, that this was a legitimate need and that they wanted to help fill that need. If it wasn't something someone wanted to fund, I tried to match their interests.

O. L. "Butch" Everett, a former board chairman at Virginia Wesleyan once told me, "Billy, I'm not interested in the English department. I hope we have people out there who are but I'm not."

"What are you interested in?" I asked.

"Tennis," he said. "That's where I'd like to help the college if you have a need there."

We had a beat-up tennis complex and we couldn't get other colleges to play us because the asphalt courts were in such bad shape. At the beginning of each season, we had to spray weed killer on the courts. There were cracks so big you could put your hand in them. Thanks to Everett, there are now eight first-rate tennis courts, and colleges that wouldn't play us now ask to come to Virginia Wesleyan for tournaments. We were also able to recruit some first-rate tennis players.

Let me see someone's checkbook and in three minutes flipping through the checkbook stubs, I'll tell you what's important to them. Money can be powerful for the people who know how to give it, and for the people who know how to ask for it and put it to good use.

My reputation was one of politely begging donors, but to me, it was an honorable reputation. I didn't like people to think I was interested in them for what they could give me and that has always bothered the heck out of me. It didn't stop me from asking because it was part of my job. Sure, some people dreaded seeing me coming down the sidewalk and no doubt said, "Oh no, here comes Greer." They also knew I valued their friendship more than their money. Reminding someone of that camaraderie made a huge difference—you could almost hear them let out a sigh of relief.

Respecting donors and would-be givers, devoting time and energy to them, and understanding their interests was as important as being humble. I'm talking about sincere, unadulterated humility. But the single most important attribute is patience and the larger the gift, the more patient I had to be. People are going to move at their own pace. They could be nudged and encouraged but I had to have thick skin and not fold up and wither away if one of my biggest benefactors slammed the door in my face. I didn't say to myself, "Oh well, they said no so I might just as well stop thinking about this project." I kept the conversation going.

Virginia Wesleyan didn't have a signature program and I dreamed that if we were known for our environmental science program that a young person in the Midwest, or elsewhere, might hear about the college and want to apply there. One time I was walking across campus with trustee Jane Batten.

"Right there is where that environmental sciences center needs to go," I said, pointing to a vacant spot and trying not to be too obnoxious. She wheeled around and said, "Billy, I know you want me to build that building but I'm not going to do it." While others might have taken no for an answer, I said to myself, "By golly, she's thinking about it."

Batten's late husband, Frank Batten, was one of the wealthiest men in the country. In 2007 he made the largest single gift in the history of the University of Virginia, dedicating $100 million to the creation of the Frank Batten School of Leadership and Public Policy. In a letter to Frank, I thanked him for his generous gift to UVa noting that a gift of that size to Virginia Wesleyan would be transformative.

Not long after, Jane Batten called when I was returning from a meeting in Richmond. She absolutely annihilated me verbally. Her anger was white hot. "What do you want us to do," she angrily asked, "give you all the money we have? You've really messed up and you'll never recover from this."

My mistake was thinking we were close enough friends that I could make a request like that. The blunder was heart-sickening. There were not many times in my life that I felt so unnerved. I was not so chummy with the Battens, or any donor, to be so impertinent. That story has stayed with me. It was a hard lesson to swallow.

Near the end of my Virginia Wesleyan career, a retirement party was hosted for Fann and me in the college dining center where we received lovely gifts and an alumni-funded $175,000 scholarship in our name. Jane Batten then talked about my dream for an environmental sciences center, noting that enrollment in our natural science department had grown by more than 100%.

"The Greer Environmental Sciences Center will help you realize your vision, Billy, of completing the quad," she announced. I gasped, along with the 350 people in the room, as a model and a video of the new center was unveiled. I couldn't stop grinning and was filled with gratitude and joy.

Working in secret, Jane Batten took it upon herself to create that center. Only a few people knew about the project they had nicknamed the "Big Fish" to keep it under wraps. Jane was symbolically saying to me, "Yeah, you once screwed up big time but I'm not holding it against you and we're going to make the program you've been dreaming about all these years happen."

Virginia Wesleyan didn't receive this gift because I was so charming. She gave the money because she knew what an impact it would have on the college, the students, and the faculty for generations. The 44,000-square-foot Greer Environmental Sciences Center was officially dedicated on September 7, 2017, which also was the college's Founders Day. Nothing could have made me prouder.

17

Looking Back, Moving Forward

On a recent spring day, I drove back to my hometown of Tifton to talk with two men whom I admired. What were their memories of "Dr. Pete" Donaldson, who was president of Abraham Baldwin Agricultural College from 1947–1961, and what made him such an indelible role model? Was he unpretentious and a man of grace with everyone? My goal was to find out what set Donaldson apart from other mentors and leaders.

The story of this great man is likely one others can relate to as they think about the men and women who helped them succeed. Like Dr. Pete, whom I sought to emulate, I've tried to be fair, kind, and respectful even though I've failed miserably at times. In hindsight, he had a lot to do with why I became a college president. He was a major shaper of young lives and when he talked about Abraham Baldwin Agricultural College you would think he was talking about Harvard. He understood the importance of diversity and his classrooms were filled with PhDs from around the world.

Driving from my home in Norfolk, Virginia, to Tifton, Georgia, there was plenty of time to reminisce as I headed down Interstates 85 and 75.

I-75 runs 337 miles through the middle of Georgia, entering the state at Lookout Mountain in the north and exiting at Lake Park in the south. The arrival of the interstate highway system in the 1950s and 1960s changed the nation's landscape, particularly the farming towns in Tift County, Georgia. For years there was a huge highway sign greeting travelers: "Tifton, Next Six Exits." Motorists would often get off the interstate and ask, "How did this little place get six exits?" The answer: we had some good politicians in this rural community whose population was no more than 6,000 in the 1950s. Today Tifton has more than 17,000 residents and has expanded its borders to the interstate, embracing all half dozen exits with hotels, gas stations, restaurants, and industries.

I suppose no one has been more proud of their hometown than I am of Tifton. Between music and news, radio station WWGS would identify itself as "the Crossroads of South Georgia." For me, it might as well have been the crossroads of the world. Even today I'm tickled when I read about someone from Tifton. While skimming through an issue of American Airlines' *American Way* magazine during a flight, I noticed a list of the best orthopedic surgeons in America. Dr. Edward W. Hellman of Tifton was one of six on that page, along with doctors from Miami, New York, and Dallas. I have no idea how the selection was made—it no doubt was paid advertising—but it nevertheless made me smile.

My first stop on that Saturday morning drive south was with Tyron Spearman. If ever there was a born and bred South Georgian, it is Tyron Spearman. He is a tall, husky man with a smile as wide as a peanut plant, a thundering voice, and a man of enormous confidence who possesses the kind of self-assuredness that draws people to him. He is the editor of the *Peanut Farm Market News* and owns the Spearman Marketing agency. At the time he also was president and CEO of the Tifton-Tift Chamber of Commerce.

Spearman laughed and cried as we dredged up memories of Dr. Pete, who had been a role model for us both. He recalled the weekly college chapel services at Abraham Baldwin College when he was a student. Once, he said, Dr. Pete stood before the whole student body and gave them a tongue-lashing.

"Students, I don't think I have ever been president of this institution when the average mid-term grades were this low. I'm ashamed of you. Now go back to your room and get your books out and I don't want to hear anything else about this." Tyron said you could hear a pin drop. Spearman recalled that 15 minutes later he was standing in the hallway of the administration building near the president's office. A state representative greeted

Donaldson and asked how things were going with the student body. "Never had a better group in my life than I've got right now," Donaldson replied with a smile.

Dr. Pete had the patience of Job and was aware that we country boys did not have good exposure to the arts, so he brought acting, theater, and opera to the campus. He crisscrossed the state recruiting students and created a boy's quartet and a girl's trio. Dr. Pete never met a microphone he didn't like. He would lead the singing at conventions and run from one side of the stage to the other waving his arms as he led the crowd in song.

"Was Dr. Pete a leader or manager?" I asked. "And which one do you think he would like to be known as?"

"He was clearly a leader," Tyron replied. "He disliked managing the organization but he very much liked talking to the students about education at Abraham Baldwin."

Dr. Pete built a powerful team of administrators. There was J. Talmadge Webb, his comptroller, who served on the Board of Directors of the ABAC Foundation for 30 years. Tom Cordell directed an adult and continuing education program thanks to a grant from the Sears and Roebuck Foundation. It was the first of its kind at a two-year college. Classes were available free to farmers. Thousands attended over the years, including former President Jimmy Carter. In its first year, 1,049 farmers attended some or all of the 20 available classes. The program was halted during World War II but started again in 1946. By then 50 courses were offered annually. Life was hard for farmers and many could barely eke out a living. Those students who could go to college got jobs picking peas and butter beans in the summer. Abraham Baldwin had its own dairy, raised beef cattle, and kept its freezers stocked with meat and vegetables. Cordell died in 1991 and the Tom M. Cordell Conference Center at Abraham Baldwin Agricultural College's Georgia Museum of Agriculture was dedicated in 2021. Webb, who died in 2010, had served under five presidents of the college and five chancellors of the University System of Georgia.

Dr. Pete was behind every success story.

My next stop was a visit with Dr. J. Frank McGill, a retired professor at the University of Georgia's Tifton campus who was known as "Mr. Peanut." My Dad said Frank McGill knew more about peanuts than anybody in the world. During his long career, the agronomist traveled to four continents and 20 countries sharing his knowledge of goobers. He donated 41 volumes of letters and progress reports to the University of Georgia library from the early 1950s. The valuable documents told the history of peanuts and peanut technology as it changed over the years when average Georgia yields increased from 800 to 3,000 pounds per acre.

McGill served as president of the American Peanut Research and Education Society and was chairman of the University of Georgia Agronomists, the U.S. Task Force on Peanut Policy, and the U.S. Peanut Improvement Working Group. He was a technical advisor to the Georgia Peanut Commission, U.S. Senate Agriculture Committee, National Peanut Council, and the National Peanut Growers Group. He had a passion not only for goobers but for education, farmers, and their families. A quintessential leader in his own right, McGill called Dr. Pete an iconic figure who, had he run for governor, certainly would have been elected.

The Georgia Peanut Commission was established, coinciding with Dr. Pete's retirement from the college. Peanut farmer A. J. Singletary of Blakely, Georgia, saw the need for the commission and invited him to be its first chair.

McGill, a member of the commission, said he watched Dr. Pete chair the first meeting and told himself, "This man knows nothing about peanuts." Several months later McGill admitted that Donaldson had not been hired because of his knowledge of the pea family plant; he had been brought on board because of his passion and integrity. He was hired because people loved and trusted him. He was hired because every farmer in peanut country knew him and believed in him. When Dr. Pete died in 1980, he left a legacy of someone who cared deeply for farmers and their families. I'm thankful I had the opportunity to talk to McGill before he died in March 2021 at the age of 95.

I've asked colleagues to think back to the men and women who have made a difference in their own careers—the leaders who instilled what it took to motivate, challenge, and encourage them as young people and as an adult. I was drawn to Dr. Pete and so many others like him because they were "real" people with no bravado or arrogance. And that made all the difference to me.

I hope that similar pathfinders will be there for generations to come. Assuming we survive the divisions tearing at this country and the specter of civil or global wars, eventually, rancor and divisiveness may be set aside. Education will be more important than ever as students learn the basics: fact from fiction, nonpartisanship, right from wrong, and the tenants of human dignity and decency.

I retired from Virginia Wesleyan in 2015 but service was in my blood. In January 2018, I became the interim president of Virginia's Eastern Shore Community College. I returned to my years-long schedule of rising before dawn to drive from my Norfolk home to the Eastern Shore across the

23-mile Chesapeake Bay Bridge Tunnel on U.S. Route 13, the main north–south highway linking the Northeast to Florida. The Eastern Shore's small towns, beaches, marshes, and wildlife set it apart from developed parts of the state like Virginia Beach, Richmond, Norfolk, or the Northern Virginia spiderweb of communities. Assateague Island, in Accomack County, is famous for its annual pony swim between Assateague and Chincoteague islands. Thousands of tourists attend the annual, nearly century-old tradition celebrated by Marguerite Henry's *Misty of Chincoteague*. Each July some ponies and foals are herded across the shallows to nearby Chincoteague and later auctioned off to maintain herd size and help fund the local fire department.

Thirty-six miles south of Chincoteague is Melfa, a flyspeck on the skinny, southern end of the Delmarva Peninsula cradled between the Chesapeake Bay and the Atlantic Ocean. It's home to Eastern Shore Community College and is one of 23 community colleges in Virginia. The school offers associate degrees, certificates, job training, and adult education.

As an administrator, I no longer taught college courses but then again aren't we all teachers? We teach every day—in offices, hallways, laboratories, over phone lines, and via email and social media. A good teacher encourages one to be more than he or she ever dreamed possible. A good teacher sees a non-mathematician and makes a mathematician. A good teacher sees a non-musician and makes a musician. A good teacher sees a non-psychologist and makes a psychologist. A good teacher knows how to give a good invitation. That is precisely why young adults arrive at college, all wide-eyed and looking for answers from us. And those answers shape them for the rest of their lives. We have an uncommon goal to reimagine higher education and the world as something bigger, better, and more significant than it has ever been.

Never stop learning. Never stop teaching. Never stop looking for mentors. No matter what our profession, we're all educators and in this topsy-turvy, uncertain world it is imperative to reinforce the basic traits of human dignity—honesty, fairness, kindness, and respectfulness. Life, indeed, is about relationships. No one can go alone. Continue learning and share that knowledge with others. Stir what you've got.

18

Where Do We Go From Here?

Everyone knows the legend of Rip Van Winkle. Before the American Revolutionary War, he wandered into New York's Catskill Mountains with his dog, Wolf, fell asleep, and didn't wake up for 20 years. When he meandered back down from the mountaintop, strangers stared at his untrimmed fingernails and his wild, foot-long white beard. His musket was rusty. His dog was gone. The portrait of England's King George III on the village tavern that he remembered had been replaced by one of George Washington, the first president of the United States. The most significant part of this familiar tale is not that Rip Van Winkle slept for two decades, but that he slept through a revolution.

I am an eternal optimist but I am also a brass knuckles realist and my greatest fear is that those of us engaged in the enterprise of higher education might find ourselves sleeping through a revolution. By that I mean we might wake up one day and see that our institutions haven't met the needs of a new generation. We get so caught up in meetings, more meetings, budgets, and all the jargon that goes with them that we fail to remember we are in the life-shaping business. Change is inevitable and we need to change with it.

We must produce intellectually adventurous graduates, who are engaged in their communities and the world and who can lead, not just by the knowledge they have acquired in college, but because they have been steeped in the principles of responsibility, honor, and mutual respect. There are those who want to turn our international political and cultural system upside down. They would have us withdraw in some sort of cloistered, hermetic void spouting lies. That is dead wrong.

I firmly believe the future of higher education is bright. Two kinds of colleges and universities likely will succeed for future generations: very wealthy institutions that not even weak presidents, boards, and faculty can kill, and smaller and less financially viable institutions that engage in strategic planning and evaluation to survive. Establishing a carefully thought-out, long-range vision and goal may sound like a no-brainer but there are colleges—and businesses—that rely on past accomplishments without thinking about what lies ahead. Could I go around the table and tell you which ones? No, but colleges and businesses are closing every year because their leaders kept doing the same things they'd always done, believing everything would be fine. It's no different for businesses. No one can amble along by resting on their laurels. And no one can predict the future. Who could have imagined that one of the biggest wolves at the door would be COVID-19, a worldwide pandemic that took the lives of millions?

Colleges and universities, companies and corporations, restaurants and retail stores big and small shuttered, some for good. In-person teaching was replaced by online courses. As the coronavirus spread and other variants burgeoned, many workers opted to stay home. Students dropped out of school. Foreign students and workers were not allowed into the country. The number of women in the workplace dwindled to its lowest level since 1988. Many school-age children were learning online and their mothers needed to be home. Others couldn't find affordable childcare. As the economy began to recover, "Help Wanted" signs were everywhere. Many feared getting COVID-19, others refused to be vaccinated when a company required the jab, and some got more emergency federal and state money by not working. Others, though, found ways to tackle the monumental pandemic stumbling block, kept their doors open with minimum staff, and were successful.

If a pandemic was not enough, independent Ukraine was invaded by Russia, obliterating cities, killing thousands, and committing atrocities not seen in Europe since World War II. Millions fled their homeland in freezing weather with little more than what they were wearing and a plastic bag with meager belongings as they sought safety in neighboring countries. Russia's unprovoked war by its dictator created unimaginable suffering and the greatest mass exodus since World War II. The United States, the European Union, the United Kingdom, Australia, New Zealand, and most of the free world countries boycotted Russia. Freedom of the press was banned in Russia, as was the word "war," as a despot sought to conquer Ukraine. The greatest fear as of this writing was that a new Cold War could transition into World War III.

Given a pandemic, a war in Eastern Europe, rising autocracies, right-wing conspiracies, and even a thwarted attempt in 2021 to overthrow our own government, it makes common sense that relationships are vital. We can't wait until we come down from a mountain 20 years from now—by then it's too late.

We've known for a long time that the country's demographics are changing, including at colleges and universities. There are more minority students. There are more young women and older adults. So we have to ask ourselves how we address the shift in student population and how will it affect an institution of higher learning.

All you have to do is count back 18 years and look at the characteristics of kids who are now in the college pipeline. One trend we see coming is young adults who don't particularly care about a degree but who are interested in welding or plumbing certificates; heating, ventilation, and air conditioning (HVAC) accreditation; or a nursing degree. They want jobs. They are more concerned about how they're going to make it financially without massive debt than they are walking across a fancy stage to receive a fancy diploma. The wave of those more interested in certificates than degrees hasn't quite gotten here yet, but it's coming.

Traditional colleges are too expensive. The wealthy can afford to pay the full price of a college education, but as middle-class families get squeezed financially, fewer will be able to afford college. We need to be ready. It's not just guesswork. The question is what are we going to do about it?

This is where serious strategic planning comes in. Sometimes we can go data crazy and allow ourselves to be overrun by consultants. We're choking on data. We have become a consultant society. I learned to beware of data overload. Some colleges go from relying on almost no analysis to putting a huge emphasis on statistics, believing if enough numbers are gathered this, that, or something else can be proved.

All these so-called experts across the country will charge big fees, come to your door, read the tea leaves and tell you exactly what you need to do.

I learned that sometimes they're absolutely necessary; often they're not. Before making decisions at Virginia Wesleyan a ton of variables were taken into consideration. I'm not trying to diminish the importance of data but there is more to making an administrative decision that will affect people now and in the future than what an analyst says.

Going to college should be one of those pivotal times in a person's life, a time when one stands between the past and the future. But when those same young men and women arrive at college as first-year students, we quickly snuff out their enthusiasm and their eagerness to learn. We say, "Please be seated; fill out this form." Thomas Jefferson wrestled with how to keep imagination alive on a college campus. He pictured an "academical village" clustered around a tree-lined lawn where students and faculty could interact and whose focal point would be a Temple of Knowledge housing the university library. "It is safer to have the whole people respectably enlightened than a few in a high state of science and the many in ignorance," he wrote.

We must encourage our students to stand out as agents of improvement. We must teach them how to withstand turbulence, especially the anxiety caused by war, a pandemic, climate change, "alternative facts," or another crisis we haven't dreamed of. We must help them seek peacefulness and find time for reflection. We will miss the possibilities of an integration of values, energy, hopes, and dreams if our educational process does not take seriously the inner dimensions of life.

My best leadership has most often occurred when I found time to quietly ponder an issue at hand. Solitude may well come in as many forms as there are people. For some, solitude is found in meditation, listening to symphonic music, or watching a breathtaking sunset over the ocean. If the experience renews one's soul that's solitude. It's where I found what being a leader meant. Thomas Merton, an American theologian, mystic, poet, social activist, and scholar of comparative religion, wrote before his death in 1968, "Every man who delights in a multitude of words, even though he says admirable things, is empty within. If you love truth, be a lover of silence" (Merton, 1969, p. 33).

Author Parker Palmer claimed we have driven the sacred out of education. We can't lose sight as educators that what we do is sacred and holy. Words like "sacred" and "holy" too often have a negative, narrow, and even fundamentalist sound to them in today's world. There is a reverence for this work. We are on this earth for a split second. Time is so fleeting that it is important that every encounter, every lecture, and every meeting counts in a special way.

Each generation of students starts clueless. To them, the world was born yesterday. They live and act as though they are attached to the society in which they live only incidentally and accidentally. They have little or no sense of the human experience through the ages, of what has been tried, of what has succeeded, and what has failed. They do not understand why they should cherish some values as opposed to others. They sometimes live as though anything is possible, without cost. Even college presidents and clergy are scared of their own shadow because they don't know what side of the political fence donors perch and they don't want to risk offending anyone. I am sounding like a horse-throated evangelist and I know it. This is our day, our time, and our weary world and the question is what are we going to do about it?

The educational skills we need must be attained through rigorous and proactive continuous learning. The time we invest in the business of leading our institutions, of the necessities of fundraising, public relations, and research cannot be ignored. We must do it all. But we must be ruthlessly compassionate educators, guiders, counselors, and leaders. We must show up. We must speak up.

The leadership principles I refer to in this book are the ones that have been the most valuable to me. While my management principles may not be the same as a Fortune 100 executive, I believe they are important for the chief executive of a company, the principal of an elementary school, the senior minister of a church, or any executive. They are key axioms—proverbs if you will—that bear repeating as our culture, world views and roles dramatically shift.

Above all: value relationships. Set an example; lead by example. Surround yourself with people who love their jobs and life. Don't stop searching until you find a career you love. Take risks, even if they make you uncomfortable. Do what is right, not what is expedient. Know when to hold 'em and when to fold 'em. Admit what you don't know. Realize that sometimes passion trumps knowledge. Hire colleagues who aren't afraid to tell you when you're wrong, and listen to them. Trust your gut. Know exactly what is expected of you. Set boundaries. Be kind. Be grateful. Never stop learning and never stop teaching. Stir what you've got.

My shrewd parents taught me not to be puffed up by my accomplishments or to be too big for my britches. As a college president, I could not abdicate authority and understood I was under a constant spotlight, even when no one was looking. I mentored others. Someone helped me; I passed it on. I didn't take life too seriously and paid attention to my family because in the end they were the only ones who cared. I laughed, even when the jokes were on me. And I was careful what I asked for because I might have gotten it. Above all, as I've said over and over—treat people the way you want to be treated. Just because you have a big title that doesn't entitle you to act like a muckety-muck, no matter if you're running a small college or if you're president of the United States. You put your pants on the same way everyone else does—one leg at a time.

The enduring joy of my life is my family. You've likely heard some people brag about a parent's successful career. Yet that mother or father was rarely home. I vowed not to be like that and was committed to participating in my children's lives, whether it was coaching sports teams, being involved in their schools, with their friends, musical groups, and being present at various activities, if they sang at a Christmas pageant or performed in any church or school play. When David was 5 years old, he fell asleep on stage as part of the cast of the play "Brigadoon" (it was, after all, past his bedtime). I wouldn't have missed that for the world!

William, Robert, and David are married to wonderful women. They all have interesting careers and contribute to their communities.

William graduated from Wofford College in Spartanburg, South Carolina, where he met his wife, Carrie Meade. They received master's degrees from Minnesota State University. William is the director of advancement for The North Cross School in Roanoke, Virginia. He loves sports, projects, and people, worked with Outward Bound setting up and running a base camp in the Florida Everglades for "at-risk youth," and loves coaching basketball and baseball. Carrie is North Cross School's gifted middle Spanish teacher and a wonderful mother to their three children: Meade Alison, born July 17, 2003; Thomas (William Thomas, IV) born December 19, 2005; and Martin Dewar, who followed on October 6, 2008. They live in Roanoke, Virginia.

Robert also graduated from Wofford College, always loved music and even in his childhood was chosen to be the lead vocalist in whatever group he performed. At the age of twelve, he was asked to sing the accompanying part for "Pie Jesu" with a soprano voice student for her graduation recital from Brevard College. Robert left teaching to start the bluegrass now turned country band "Town Mountain," which has been described by *Rolling Stone* magazine as one of "Ten New Artists You Need to Know." The group has played from coast to coast and internationally. His wife, Rachel Simmons, graduated from law school in May 2022.

David graduated from Millsaps College in Jackson, Mississippi where he majored in geology and played basketball for the college. He went on to earn a earned a master's degree from the University of North Carolina at Chapel Hill. When David arrived in Chapel Hill, he ran into a childhood friend from Brevard. He called us reporting, "Guess who I saw tonight—Amanda Womble, and she is looking good!" He married Amanda in October 2005, and they live in Chapel Hill with their sons Polk Truan, born April 25, 2011, and Watson Parker, born December 28, 2013. David is the director of development for the Morehead Cain Foundation, and Amanda is a doctor of nursing anesthesia practice and works as a certified registered nurse anesthetist.

Fann and I are aware it is up to our three children and our five precious grandchildren to be good stewards of this planet, and to build on a legacy of giving, integrity, and kindness. We're proud of each of our children's accomplishments, but most of all the people they have become.

It hit me one day recently that I really am retired. That doesn't mean I want to sit in a rocking chair on the front porch; I never want to stop learning and growing.

I'm not a doomsayer or a Pollyanna, but I am sanguine knowing many idealists care deeply about this country. There comes a time when we have to say enough is enough. That time is now and I hope and pray it won't be too late because our democratic institutions, our nation's values, our integrity, the world in which we live and our very lives are at stake. When we don't vote or actively participate in civic discourse, we lose our voice and give up our personal authority.

I am reminded of Elie Wiesel's 1986 Nobel Laureate acceptance speech which is as timely today as it was more than three decades ago. He had been asked by a boy what he had done with his life:

> That I have tried to keep the memory alive, that I have tried to fight those who would forget. Because if we forget, we are guilty, we are accomplices. And then I explained to him how naïve we were, that the world did know and remained silent. And that is why I swore never to be silent whenever or wherever human beings endure suffering and humiliation. We must take sides. Neutrality helps the oppressor, never the victim. Silence encourages the tormentor, never the tormented. Sometimes we must interfere. When human lives are endangered, when human dignity is in jeopardy, national borders and sensitivities become irrelevant. Wherever men and women are persecuted because of their race, religion, or political views, that place must—at that moment—become the center of the universe. (Wiesel, 1986, n.p.)

Fann and I have tried our best to leave the world in a better place "toward the place where our deep gladness meets the world's deep need," as Parker Palmer (1999, p. 36) so elegantly wrote.

Like so many of us, we are shaped and molded by our upbringing, our education, and our careers. Our dreams brought Fann and me to churches and colleges, and communities ringed by golden fields, rugged mountains, and the soothing waves of an ocean. We had big dreams but we all must dream big. We must be determined to hold onto those dreams and find the energy and good judgment to see them become realities. I needed all the help, encouragement, wisdom, and prayers to make that happen.

We all do.

References

Barclay, W. (1975a). *The gospel of Luke.* Saint Andrew Press.

Barclay, W. (1975b). *The gospel of John, Volume II.* Saint Andrew Press.

Barclay, W. (1987). *The plain man's book of prayers.* William Collins & Sons. (original work published 1959)

Dillon, D., & Bartholomew, L. H. (2015). Tennessee whiskey [Recorded by Chris Staleton]. On *Traveller* [Album]. Mercury Records.

Kula, I. (2006). *Yearnings: Embracing the sacred messiness of life.* Hachette Books.

Merten, T. (1969). *Contemplative prayer.* Herder and Herder.

Nerburn, K. (1994). *Neither wolf nor dog.* New World Library.

Palmer, P. J. (1999). *Let your life speak: Listening for the voice of vocation.* John Wiley & Sons.

Pearson, R. (1998, September 14). *Washington Post.* p. A1

Schlitz, D. (1978). The gambler [Recorded by Kenny Rogers]. On *The gambler* [Album]. United Artists.

Tillich, P. (1948). *The shaking of the foundations.* Charles Scribner's Sons.

Wiesel, E. (1986). *Acceptance speech.* NobelPrize.org. https://www.nobelprize.org/prizes/peace/1986/wiesel/acceptance-speech